ERNEST J. GAINES

ERNEST J. GAINES

A Critical Companion

Karen Carmean

CRITICAL COMPANIONS TO POPULAR CONTEMPORARY WRITERS
Kathleen Gregory Klein, Series Editor

Greenwood Press
Westport, Connecticut • London

Library of Congress Cataloging-in-Publication Data

Carmean, Karen.
    Ernest J. Gaines : a critical companion / Karen Carmean.
        p.   cm.—(Critical companions to popular contemporary
    writers, ISSN 1082–4979)
    Includes bibliographical references (p.   ) and index.
    ISBN 0–313–30286–3 (alk. paper)
    1. Gaines, Ernest J., 1933–   —Criticism and interpretation.
    2. Afro-Americans in literature.   3. Louisiana—In literature.
    I. Title.   II. Series.
    PS3557.A355Z62   1998
    813'.54–DC21   97–48578

British Library Cataloguing in Publication Data is available.

Library of Congress Catalog Card Number: 97–48578
ISBN: 0–313–30286–3
ISSN: 1082–4979

First published in 1998

Greenwood Press, 88 Post Road West, Westport, CT 06881
An imprint of Greenwood Publishing Group, Inc.

Printed in the United States of America

The paper used in this book complies with the
Permanent Paper Standard issued by the National
Information Standards Organization (Z39.48–1984).

10 9 8 7 6 5 4 3 2 1

For My Parents

Jean Lillian Bell
and
Thomas A. Carmean
in
loving memory

.

Contents

Series Foreword

The authors who appear in the series Critical Companions to Popular Contemporary Writers are all best-selling writers. They do not simply have one successful novel, but a string of them. Fans, critics, and specialist readers eagerly anticipate their next book. For some, high cash advances and breakthrough sales figures are automatic; movie deals often follow. Some writers become household names, recognized by almost everyone.

But, their novels are read one by one. Each reader chooses to start and, more importantly, to finish a book because of what she or he finds there. The real test of a novel is in the satisfaction its readers experience. This series acknowledges the extraordinary involvement of readers and writers in creating a best-seller.

The authors included in this series were chosen by an Advisory Board composed of high school English teachers and high school and public librarians. They ranked a list of best-selling writers according to their popularity among different groups of readers. For the first series, writers in the top-ranked group who had received no book-length, academic, literary analysis (or none in at least the past ten years) were chosen. Because of this selection method, Critical Companions to Popular Contemporary Writers meets a need that is being addressed nowhere else. The success of these volumes as reported by reviewers, librarians, and teachers led to an expansion of the series mandate to include some writers with wide critical attention—Toni Morrison, John Irving, and Maya Angelou, for example—to extend the usefulness of the series.

The volumes in the series are written by scholars with particular expertise in analyzing popular fiction. These specialists add an academic focus to the popular success that these writers already enjoy.

The series is designed to appeal to a wide range of readers. The general reading public will find explanations for the appeal of these well-known writers. Fans will find biographical and fictional questions answered. Students will find literary analysis, discussions of fictional genres, carefully organized introductions to new ways of reading the novels, and bibliographies for additional research. Whether browsing through the book for pleasure or using it for an assignment, readers will find that the most recent novels of the authors are included.

Each volume begins with a biographical chapter drawing on published information, autobiographies or memoirs, prior interviews, and, in some cases, interviews given especially for this series. A chapter on literary history and genres describes how the author's work fits into a larger literary context. The following chapters analyze the writer's most important, most popular, and most recent novels in detail. Each chapter focuses on one or more novels. This approach, suggested by the Advisory Board as the most useful to student research, allows for an in-depth analysis of the writer's fiction. Close and careful readings with numerous examples show readers exactly how the novels work. These chapters are organized around three central elements: plot development (how the story line moves forward), character development (what the reader knows of the important figures), and theme (the significant ideas of the novel). Chapters may also include sections on generic conventions (how the novel is similar or different from others in its same category of science, fantasy, thriller, etc.), narrative point of view (who tells the story and how), symbols and literary language, and historical or social context. Each chapter ends with an "alternative reading" of the novel. The volume concludes with a primary and secondary bibliography, including reviews.

The alternative readings are a unique feature of this series. By demonstrating a particular way of reading each novel, they provide a clear example of how a specific perspective can reveal important aspects of the book. In the alternative reading sections, one contemporary literary theory—way of reading, such as feminist criticism, Marxism, new historicism, deconstruction, or Jungian psychological critique—is defined in brief, easily comprehensible language. That definition is then applied to the novel to highlight specific features that might go unnoticed or be understood differently in a more general reading. Each volume defines two or three specific theories, making them part of the reader's understanding of how diverse meanings may be constructed from a single novel.

Taken collectively, the volumes in the Critical Companions to Popular Contemporary Writers series provide a wide-ranging investigation of the complexities of current best-selling fiction. By treating these novels seriously as both literary works and publishing successes, the series demonstrates the potential of popular literature in contemporary culture.

Kathleen Gregory Klein
Southern Connecticut State University

Acknowledgments

Writing is an essentially solitary pursuit, but I have been most fortunate in having company. I want to thank Georg Gaston, whose enthusiasm for this project and editing skills spurred me on and improved the manuscript. I'd also like to thank both Barbara Rader and Kathleen Gregory Klein for offering me the opportunity to write about one of my favorite authors.

1

The Life of Ernest J. Gaines

Ernest J. Gaines says that he "came from a place where people sat around and chewed sugar-cane and roasted sweet potatoes and peanuts in the ashes and sat on ditch banks and told tales and sat on porches and went into the swamps and went into the fields—that's where I came from" (Lowe, 224). This place, which seems almost magical in its remove from the reality of most lives, had its own, quite authentic, rhythms and textures. Gaines has often described his childhood home as an ideal background for a writer (119). Citing Louisiana's distinctive cultural mixes, its caste system, its Catholic-Protestant background, and its entrenched plantation system lasting into the 1950s, he calls Louisiana the "most romantic and interesting of all southern states" (68). Gaines was born on River Lake Plantation near Oscar, Louisiana, in Point Coupee Parish on January 15, 1933. His parents, Manuel and Adrienne Gaines, worked as sharecroppers on the same plantation where their forebearers had labored as slaves. Adrienne was sixteen years old when her son was born. Ernest James, called EJ by his family, was the oldest of the seven children Adrienne had with Manuel Gaines. Though he recalls many instances from his childhood in vivid detail, Gaines seems to have few memories of his father, who abandoned his family when EJ was around eight years old. To support her family, Adrienne continued field labor before moving to New Orleans in search of work.

The Great Depression lingered through the 1940s in the South, where limited education and job opportunities were the rule for most citizens, especially blacks. The growing Gaines family lived in the workers' quarters, formerly the slave quarters, in a two-room house which had seen no modern improvements. Before a water hydrant was installed in front of his grandmother's home, all water had to be drawn from wells. Heat came from the kitchen stove and a fireplace. There was no electricity. While she worked, Adrienne left her children in the care of their great aunt, Miss Augusteen Jefferson, her maternal grandfather's sister. Though crippled by an undiagnosed condition, Aunt Teen, as the family called her, provided not only care and discipline but set an example of courage that would mark Gaines all his life. Without complaint she managed to sew, cook, and clean; then she would crawl to her garden. She planted in EJ her love of the earth, an appreciation of growing things, and a lifelong admiration of her moral example. "What I learned from her was a tremendous amount of discipline," Gaines recalls. Like James in his story "The Sky Is Gray," EJ's job was to assist Aunt Augusteen, rising early to cut wood for the stove, draw water, and set an example for his younger siblings. While survival demanded hard labor, life required some respite; this they would find in their evening discussions. Because of Aunt Augusteen's disability and her natural hospitality, their home proved to be a local magnet, where members of the small plantation community gathered on the porch steps, swapping news and stories. Serving their guests coffee or water, Ernest listened to stories from an early age and absorbed their language. Of all the people in his life, Gaines believes Aunt Augusteen has had the greatest influence on him and his writing career.

Growing up during the Great Depression, Gaines, like many rural children, was put to work early. From the age of eight he was in the fields, picking cotton and gathering Irish potatoes for fifty cents a day. Later, he would be sent to cut wood in the swamps. Gaines says, "it was hard and tough being the oldest child. I had to go into the swamps to cut wood for the stove as well as fireplace. When you're a twelve-year-old kid trying to pull a saw for half a day, it's about the most cruel thing you can do to somebody" (Lowe, 286). Most of this labor took place during the seven months when school was not held for black students. In those days, education for blacks was distinctly separate and inferior. Gaines attended elementary school in a nearby plantation church from October, after the cotton harvest, until April, when planting season began. He was an able pupil whose skills were often put to use by the older, mostly illiterate residents of the plantation. They would ask Ernest to write letters to friends and relatives. Prodded by Aunt Teen, Gaines "would go to these people and read their letters for them and write their letters for them. In most cases they didn't know how to form the letter. They'd give me a little piece of paper, you know, those small, narrow tablets and pencil and say, 'tell Viney' or 'tell Clara I'm all right. We're doing ok., and the garden's all right.' Something like that. Then I would have to form the letter. I'd just write it, and rewrite it, and rewrite it until I got it right. Then I'd read it back to them" (121). Thus, from his earliest efforts at writing, Ernest Gaines would learn to produce multiple drafts until crafting a satisfactory version of a story.

In 1945, Gaines began attending St. Augustine, a black Catholic school in nearby New Roads. Since there were no school buses to transport black children, he had to hitchhike or catch a country bus. Often, the plantation owner, who was also the sheriff, would drive him to school. When EJ offered to shine his shoes to repay this service, the sheriff refused, telling the impressionable boy that he didn't have to shine anyone's shoes for a living. St. Augustine provided three years of additional education, through the seventh grade. During this time, Gaines began writing and directing plays performed in the plantation church.

In 1947, Adrienne followed her second husband, Ralph Colar, to Vallejo, California, north of San Francisco. Though he once worked on nearby Parlange Plantation, Colar had joined the Merchant Marine. Adrienne found work in a factory and they began saving money to bring the children who had been left behind in Louisiana. As the oldest of a still-growing family (Adrienne would have five children with Ralph Colar) and as someone without access to high school, Gaines joined his parents in Vallejo in 1948. Now fifteen years old, he had absorbed the deep sense of community on River Lake Plantation but was also ready for an adventure. The move to northern California changed the direction of his life. "Had I left five years earlier, I would not have had enough experiences. Had I stayed five years longer, I would have been broken— in prison, dead, insane. . . . I left at the very best time to leave. I knew the quarter and the plantation and the small town. I knew the Catholics, the Baptists, the Creoles, the mulattoes, the problems between black and white" (Lowe, 279). Gaines believes that leaving Louisiana precisely when he did was "the best thing that ever happened" to him (176).

But as exciting as the move was, for the first time in his life, young Gaines was completely out of his element. So he took the advice from his new friends seriously: "Don't tell anyone you're from the country. Tell them you're from the city." Gaines recalls that for almost two years after he moved to California when anyone asked where he was from he'd say, " 'Oh, I came from New Orleans.' When they'd say name the street you lived on, I'd say 'Canal Street?' Everybody knew it was a damned lie. Finally I realized, hey man, you gotta be what you are. So, I thought, well, this is what I am. This is all I am" (Lowe, 224). Living with his parents in a multiracial government housing project, Gaines made friends with people from all ethnic backgrounds: Asian, Hispanic, and Caucasian. When his parents found an apartment in downtown Vallejo, however, he discovered action in the streets. His stepfather, a disciplinarian with firm ideas about performance, ordered EJ to find a more useful investment of his time than loitering on street corners.

Thus, at sixteen and lonely for his friends and family in Louisiana, Ernest Gaines went looking for them in the Vallejo Public Library. It was his first experience in a library, since their use in the South was reserved for whites only, but it quickly became his refuge. At first he sampled books, taking them off the shelves and randomly reading a page or paragraph. Then he discovered the fiction section and began a futile hunt for the people and places he missed. Willa Cather and John Steinbeck's works were interesting, but their characters weren't the people he knew. Disappointed in the strained, stereotypical characters he found in various books, he decided to write his own story. "I wrote it in one summer, the summer I was sixteen. It was probably the worst novel, the worst number of pages that anyone could possibly call a novel" (Lowe, 59). Gaines laboriously wrote out a love story "between a fair-skinned girl and a dark-skinned guy—he's Protestant; she's Catholic—and the conflict they had" (265). He based his character named Catherine on a child he had known in Louisiana whose parents disapproved of any contact with dark-skinned people. Then Gaines nagged his mother into renting a typewriter. Believing that a book manuscript had to look like a book, he carefully cut typing paper in half and picked out the letters one by one while he babysat his infant brother Michael. He called his story "A Little Stream," and when he finished typing it out, he mailed it to a New York publisher. This story, which bears the outline of *Catherine Carmier*, was quickly returned to Gaines, who burned the manuscript in his disappointment.

In 1951, Gaines graduated from high school. Since he had no money for college, he began taking courses at Vallejo Junior College, which was then free to residents. After graduating in 1953, Gaines was drafted by the U.S. Army. After his basic training at Fort Ord, California, he spent six months at Camp Chaffee, Arkansas, before going to Guam. After two years, he used his GI Bill to complete a bachelor's degree at San Francisco State College, supplementing his $110 monthly government stipend with money earned by working in a post office and for a printer. Rather than focusing on literature, he chose to study language arts with an emphasis on creative writing. "My minor was English lit, but my major was language art. You have some playwriting and direction, speech, journalism, a little of all the language arts" (Lowe, 195). He believes that his instructors "took an interest in me very early. They singled me out and gave me a lot of help. I was the only black in the class. There must have been about twenty to twenty-five people, and I was the only black. They were very encouraging" (52). He struggled with a conventional course in essay writing until he persuaded his instructor to let him substitute fiction. Not only did he pass the course, his writing efforts finally saw print. Gaines published several stories in the college literary magazine, *Transfer*. Two of these stories, "The Turtles" and "The Boy in the Double-Breasted Suit," would be included in his subsequent application for a creative writing fellowship application to Stanford University.

When he graduated from San Francisco State, Gaines gave himself ten years to make his name as a writer. Since he had no money for graduate education, he took a job and worked on his third story as part of his application for the Wallace Stegner Creative Writing Award. He won, and Stanford gave him "money and time to work" (Lowe, 52). More than that, his instructors at Stanford gave him a good deal of constructive feedback on his work. To illustrate how to achieve various effects, they studied the works of experimental writers. Though he had read widely in the Vallejo Public Library, he now learned to read deeply, meaning that he learned to pay attention to technique. Hemingway, Faulkner, Turgenev, Chekhov, Flaubert, Joyce—these writers, and more, had much to show Gaines about constructing stories. Again, he proved a perceptive student.

Continuing to work on his short stories, Gaines published "A Long Day in November" in 1959. But a New York editor visiting one of Gaines's creative writing classes advised him that there was no money in short stories. Thus, determined to make his living as a writer, Gaines cast about for an idea for a novel. His previous, failed attempt surfaced. This time he would imbue the story with the techniques he had been taught. During the five years of work on the novel he would call *Catherine Carmier*, he would wrestle through these techniques until he developed his own.

He set about his task in a businesslike manner, working every day of the week: "I get up at 6:30 or 7 A.M., eat a little food, go out for a four to five mile walk, come back, shower and then stare at that damn desk" (Lowe, 142). Writing five hours a day, five days a week, Gaines enforced a discipline that would continue regardless of success. This working discipline, established so early in his career, has carried over to the present. Now, he usually writes two longhand versions, the first one quickly, the second more slowly, before moving to a typewriter. After two more typewritten versions, he considers that he has a "first" draft, something to show his agent. This draft will go through additional changes, according to the advice of his editor.

Gaines began working with editor Dorthea Oppenheimer in 1959, and when she decided to become a literary agent, she represented his business interests. More than simply business, however, Oppenheimer developed a close working relationship with Gaines, who has described her as his "most important" reader: "She would suggest things and it was her opinion I appreciated more than anyone else's" (Lowe, 213). Gaines listened to Oppenheimer's advice about more than problems with his work. When she advised him to leave a publisher who had not promoted his novels as forcefully as Oppenheimer thought he ought to, Gaines would follow her direction. Their mutual faith in each other was an important supporting factor in Gaines's literary career, their special relationship ending only with Oppenheimer's death in 1987.

Gaines's only publications between 1959 and 1964, when *Catherine Carmier* was published, were his stories "Like a Tree" in 1962 and "The Sky Is Gray" in 1963. The former was inspired by Faulkner's use of multiple narrators in *As I Lay Dying*. Gaines would return to the use of multiple narrators in *A Gathering of Old Men*, and he would use the character of Aunt Fe from this story as the basis of Miss Jane Pittman. "The Sky Is Gray" was written as Gaines's response to James Meredith's courageous attempts to integrate the University of Mississippi. These were lean years for Gaines, who supported himself through part-time jobs, including one delivering mail at an insurance company. He vividly remembers how "I used to sneak into the bathroom and write on paper towels. My boss would kick the door and yell, 'Get back to work!' And I'd say, 'Don't you know there's a genius at work in here?' " (Lowe, 293). Living in a tiny apartment and on a diet of pork and beans and hot dogs, Gaines recalls thinking, "Here I was, the first male in my family to go to college, and I was living like a bum" (295). But the discipline taught him by Aunt Teen and enforced by his stepfather had become a part of his being. Thus, every morning Gaines rose to write before going to work at jobs he disliked in the afternoon. Living on $175 a month, he acknowledges that his life "was hand to mouth. But 99 percent of the people who write have gone through that. No one twisted my arm to be a writer, I chose it" (83).

By 1963, Gaines felt stalled. His writing seemed stale, and his life in San Francisco seemed to have assumed a holding pattern. First he considered moving to Mexico to join friends. But when he read about James Meredith's composure in the face of the media lights and political theatre staged by Mississippi Governor Ross Barnet and U.S. Attorney General Robert Kennedy, Gaines changed his plans: "I kept thinking and thinking about this brave, very brave man—and told myself that if James Meredith can go through all this—not only for himself but for his race (and that included me as well)—then I, too, should go back to the source that I was trying to write about" ("Miss Jane and I," 31–32). So in January of 1963, Gaines began a six-month sojourn in Baton Rouge, a sojourn that he credits with reinvigorating his uncertain writing career. Refreshing his sense of place, language, and character, this visit furthered Gaines's creative energies as he completed work on *Catherine Carmier*.

His $1,500 advance for the novel long since spent, Gaines hoped that *Catherine Carmier* would enjoy a modest success. Its reception was disappointing since the novel was barely reviewed at all, and then without much enthusiasm. Expecting a continuation of the protest tradition, reviewers failed to grasp the more subtle handling of racial issues Gaines dramatized. Despite his disappointment, Gaines moved ahead, putting his efforts into work about San Francisco's bohemian life. As the site of a variety of countercultural movements and as a gathering spot for artists and intellectuals, San Francisco seemed a perfect fictional setting. But though Gaines loved the romantic flavor of his adopted city, he discovered that he couldn't write about it, at least not to his satisfaction. His four unpublished novels set in San Francisco suggest that he didn't easily abandon his notion, but he has candidly described this work as "unpublishable."

Supported by a National Endowment for the Arts Study Award, Gaines pursued other publishing opportunities. The Dial Press gave him a two-book contract; it would publish Gaines's short stories if he would write a novel. Listening to blues recordings one afternoon, a fresh idea cystallized for Gaines. He decided to take the character Proctor Lewis from his story "Three Men" and place him in the tenuous situation Lightnin' Hopkins sings about in "Mr. Tim Moore's Farm." Seven months later, Gaines had produced *Of Love and Dust*, published in 1967.

Everything seemed to come together for this novel. Its focus on inter-racial love affairs had a certain popular appeal, and Gaines's own mastery of technique now seemed evident. Though the critical notice was slight, it was nevertheless more positive. For example, Sara Blackburn, writing for *Nation*, described the book as "serious and powerful."

With the publication of *Bloodline* in 1968, Gaines's presence on the contemporary American fiction scene seemed evident, though reviewers frequently overlooked his subtle artistry. Placing him with his contemporary African American writers, reviewers wrote about Gaines's theme of manhood, often failing to detect other, more subtle ideas. Laurence LaFore, writing for the *New York Times Book Review*, classified Gaines as a "naturalist" who deals with "unprivileged people in a world that has only one dimension in time" before going on to praise his technical control and accurate ear. Gaines largely ignored his critical reception and continued writing.

By now the spirit of a 110-year-old woman had taken over his imagination, and, undeterred by the unsettled politics of the late 1960s, Gaines would shut out the voices of protest to listen to Miss Jane Pittman. Supported in 1970 by a Rockefeller Grant, he continued working on an idea he describes as having its inception on the porch of Aunt Augusteen's house on River Lake Plantation. The actual writing took place over a number of years following a conversation Gaines had with his friend Al Aubert, a historian at Southern University. Gaines remembers that he focused their discussion by saying, "Let's talk about twelve things that could have happened nationally that a woman who lived to be 110 years old might be able to recall" (Lowe, 94). After assembling a list, Gaines began research—histories, conversations, and archival material. Moving between San Francisco and Baton Rouge, he pieced together a background before he determined voice. For this he relied on *Lay My Burden Down*, a collection of Works Progress Administration interviews conducted with former slaves, and his own conversations with people. While he was in Louisiana, Gaines "would go out into the fields and talk to the people, talk about Huey Long, talk about the flood, talk about Angola State Prison, talk about Jackson Mental Institution. We talked about everything" (94). His combination of firsthand research combined with historical details would give a sense of authentic history to what has become his most famous novel.

In 1971, Gaines accepted a post as writer in residence at Denison University in Granville, Ohio. If his reputation as an American writer had seemed tenuous, the publication of *The Autobiography of Miss Jane Pittman* that year secured for him a firm place in American literature. Though some reviewers continued to categorize Gaines as a "black" writer, others showed more wisdom in perceiving how this novel—and its author—transcended limiting categories. *The Autobiography of Miss Jane Pittman* became a best-selling novel and was nominated for a Pulitzer Prize. Capitalizing on the enthusiastic reception of the film adaptation of Alex Haley's book *Roots*, CBS purchased film rights for a television movie. Gaines sold the television rights for $50,000. While *The Autobiography of Miss Jane Pittman* failed to win a Pulitzer, the film version swept the Emmy Awards. Cicely Tyson won for her performance as Miss Jane, and the film's director, screenwriter, and music composer also walked away with awards. Ernest Gaines labored on. He recalls *"Miss Jane* carried me on her back for a long time" (Lowe, 143).

He welcomed the literary awards following *The Autobiography of Miss Jane Pittman*—a Guggenheim Fellowship, the California Gold Medal, the Louisiana Library Association Award, and the Black Academy of Arts and Letters Award. But the financial respite gained from the publication and prizes of *The Autobiography of Miss Jane Pittman* and "A Long Day in November" as a children's book melted away during the next years as Gaines struggled with his most difficult writing project. He began work on a piece entitled "The House and the Field" before abandoning it for *In My Father's House*. During seven years of writing and rewriting, Gaines wrestled with this novel. His $20,000 advance was practically forgotten by 1978, when *In My Father's House* was finally published; Gaines wondered about his ability to support himself as a writer. Temporary stints as a writer in residence failed to provide a financial margin of comfort. Even after the publication of *A Gathering of Old Men* in 1983, Gaines felt financial pressure. When an injury from a fall required expensive knee surgery, he knew he needed a steady source of income.

Gaines had been earning income as a writer in residence at a number of colleges and universities, including Denison University, the University of Arkansas, and Whittier College, but these were irregularly timed and the income derived from his appearances varied. Then the University of Southwestern Louisiana (USL) offered him a permanent arrangement: "I came down in '81 and spent a year, and they asked me if I would like to come back every year for one semester, and I said okay. At that same time, the University of Houston asked me to do the same thing, to teach one semester on alternate years, and I thought I could teach one semester at Houston on one year and one semester at USL on the next. I could write the rest of the time" (Lowe, 190). This plan seemed a solution until

1983, when USL offered Gaines a tenured position and a house near campus: "Good Lord!" was Gaines's response, "now I'll have to call the people in Houston and tell them that I'm not coming back to Texas" (190). Gaines agreed to teach fall semesters at USL so that he could return to San Francisco to write. Now, he offers a graduate course in creative writing and selects about fifteen students on their writing merit. As a teacher, Gaines's goal is to help students "with their craft. I try to stay away from philosophies and what their symbols are supposed to symbolize" (247).

In 1984, the film version of *A Gathering of Old Men* was made for television. Volker Schlondorff, the notable German director, filmed it on location in Thibodaux. Now living in Lafayette, Gaines had the opportunity to observe the filming first hand. Understanding that film is a very different medium from writing and that he had no control over the film version, Gaines went along with the many, often necessary changes in adapting a novel to film. Though at first doubtful about the casting of Louis Gossett, Jr. as Mathu, Gaines quickly saw that Gossett could bring off the role. Ultimately, though, he believes that whatever the quality of the film, "people will watch it and go out and buy the book" (Lowe, 204). By this time, three of Gaines's works had been adapted for television films, "The Sky Is Gray" being the third.

Gaines now seemed settled into a pattern of commuting to Louisiana to teach for half a year and then returning to San Francisco to write, punctuated by conferences, book signings, and guest appearances. But his life, never dull to begin with, had more surprises in store. In 1988, Gaines met Dianne Saulney at the Miami International Book Fair. An assistant county attorney in Dade County, Florida, she was the mother of adult children from a previous marriage and had family ties to Louisiana which she would strengthen through Gaines. After five years of courtship, Gaines married Dianne in May 1993. He had already enjoyed a good year, beginning with a documentary on the plantation culture of his youth, entitled *Ernest J. Gaines: Louisiana Stories*, which aired first on Louisiana Public Broadcasting and then on PBS stations throughout the nation. Then *A Lesson Before Dying* was released in April to enthusiastic reviews; it would win the National Book Critics Circle Award and be nominated for a Pulitzer Prize. Then, while relaxing in their Miami condominium following his marriage, Gaines was notified by the John D. and Catherine T. MacArthur Foundation that he had won a "genius grant." These unrestricted awards, among the most coveted in the United States, are given to people the foundation finds notable for their originality, dedication, and self-direction. After thirty years of writing, Gaines's work finally earned a significant amount of money. His award of $335,000 ensured a level of comfort unprecedented in his life. He accepted with gratitude and reservation: "Whenever too much good happens, I'm afraid. I hate to be pessimistic, but I think that life is balance. A lot of people are saying, 'You deserve this; you've never received this kind of recognition before.' But I'm getting so much now. And some kind of way, the Old Man balances" (Lowe, 277).

2

Genres

Ernest Gaines has never been concerned about his "place" in American literature: "I don't give a damn what category people put me in. If they buy my books, they can put me in any category they want" (Lowe, 141–42). While literary labels might seem meaningless to a writer, they sometimes prove useful to teachers and students. Given the varieties of literary expression, placing a literary figure often helps readers to understand how one writer relates to others of similar fictional forms, interests, times, and places. "Genre" is a French word literally translating as "type." Like many literary terms, it has a number of applications. When written literature was comparatively young, the word referred to specific kinds of literary expression such as comedy, tragedy, epic, or lyric. Its more contemporary application refers to different literary forms such as story, poem, drama, or novel. Within these literary categories, however, are further designations based on subject matter, period, theme, style, ethnic origin, or even geographical region. Whenever he is asked about what kind of writer he is, Gaines offers the following: "I see myself as a writer and I happen to have been born here [in Louisiana]. I was born black. . . . I'm a different writer from, say, Faulkner, and I'm a different writer from a lot of black writers" (228–29). These differences may be used to define Gaines's place and to illustrate what makes him a great fiction writer instead of a merely gifted one.

Gaines often depicts characters who don't see clearly, unlike their invisible creator, and this tendency underlines one fact about his fiction. It is not autobiographical. Though Gaines clearly evokes the place and time of his youth in Louisiana, though all of his works are set in the rural St. Raphael Parish, and though he draws upon his own experiences in his fiction, the works themselves are neither patterned on his life nor centered on a fictional alter ego, as is the case of, for example, Pat Conroy. Instead, Gaines invites readers into a personally created world that looks as if it might reflect his own experience but represents an experience that encompasses those of many. Set in the past, most of his work seems contemporaneous because it inhabits its own time. Even Gaines's most apparently autobiographical work, "The Sky Is Gray," is not, ultimately, autobiographical. Gaines has commented directly on making too much of the autobiographical element: "In 'The Sky Is Gray' now, much of what little James goes through—and my middle name is James, you know—I went through. But it's not me" (Lowe, 182). His work is not autobiographical because it so artfully condenses experience, develops specific themes, and completes them in ways that are satisfying without calling attention to a message. Gaines's work, then, is artful without being artificial. He will use parts of people, places, and experiences he knows and then transform these into fictional representations that literally transcend all particulars.

Additionally, it's not accurate to say that Ernest Gaines is merely a black writer. He is a writer who happens to be black. As he says, "I never think of myself as number one a black writer, quote black, or Louisiana black, but as a writer who happens to draw from his environment what his life is, what heritage is" (Lowe, 229). Early in his career, reviewers, wanting to place Gaines conveniently, tried to group his work with what they were already familiar with, namely the novels of Richard Wright, Ralph Ellison, and James Baldwin. This presented obvious problems, since Wright, writing in the 1930s and 1940s, came from an entirely different experience, as did Ellison and Baldwin. Their works were notably angry, obviously political, and urban; in fact, their work neatly fit into the "protest" tradition in African American literature. Writing during the politically charged 1960s and 1970s, Gaines listened to a lot of criticism that his fiction wasn't sufficiently angry or political. He ignored it: "I stuck to my ground—to writing my particular book. I felt I had already set the goals for my writing, and I intended to go on. I followed the work of the sixties, read a lot of it—criticized a lot of it. But I established my direction before they started" (150).

These goals were established by the time he finished his work at Stan-

ford, and they can be traced to the kind of instruction Gaines received
and the kinds of literary influences he has acknowledged in his work.
When asked to list his literary influences, Gaines includes Faulkner's *The
Sound and the Fury* and *As I Lay Dying*, Hemingway's stories, Turgenev's
Fathers and Sons, Twain's *The Adventures of Huckleberry Finn*, Crane's *The
Red Badge of Courage*, Chekhov's stories, de Maupassant's stories, Flaubert's *Madame Bovary*, Cervantes' *Don Quixote*, Gogol's *Dead Souls*, Joyce's
Dubliners, Fitzgerald's *The Great Gatsby*, Tolstoy, and Shakespeare (Lowe,
64). These works were routinely taught in most literature programs during the 1950s and 1960s, programs that rarely included any works by
African American writers. Gaines recalls that in his own experience only
one black writer, Richard Wright, was even mentioned. But Wright's
works, for example *Native Son* and *Black Boy*, were never taught. The
writers held up as models were primarily Ernest Hemingway, William
Faulkner, and James Joyce, all stylistic innovators. Gaines learned specific
lessons from each: "I learned much about dialogue from Faulkner, especially when we're dealing with our southern dialects. I learned
rhythms from Gertrude Stein, learned to put a complete story in a day
from Joyce's *Ulysses* and Tolstoy's "The Death of Ivan Ilych" (208). Hemingway's influence is evident in Gaines's use of understatement, in his
dramatic rendering of character through gesture or dialogue, and in his
economic use of language and repetition. Gaines also recognizes Hemingway's influence in his thematic concerns: "I feel that Hemingway was
writing more about blacks than he was really about whites when he was
using the grace under pressure theme. I see that Hemingway usually
put his people in a moment where they must have grace under pressure,
and I've often looked at black life, not only as a moment, but more as
something constant, everyday. This is what my characters must come
through" (207).

By the time Gaines discovered a lengthy and rich African American
literary tradition in the late sixties, his style was already his own. He has
expressed admiration for numerous writers, including Alice Walker,
James Alan McPherson, James Baldwin, and Ralph Ellison. But he singles
out Jean Toomer's work, *Cane*, as especially powerful, and believes that
this work made an impression on the very writers whose work influenced his style: "I discovered *Cane* in the sixties. I thought it was so
poetic—you know, Sherwood Anderson knew about that book, and I'm
almost certain that he mentioned it to Gertrude Stein and Hemingway
because of those little things in Hemingway's first collection of stories,
In Our Time—he has those little breaks between each one of those stories,

and I wonder if he didn't get that from having read Toomer's *Cane*; and, of course, *Cane* came out much earlier" (Lowe, 317). Gaines shares with Toomer a celebration of and sensuous response to the land and the appreciative perspective of one who, having lived in another region, can see anew. *Cane* is singled out from all the rest as Gaines's favorite novel by a black writer.

As important as reading is to any writer, Gaines also acknowledges other, less obvious artistic influences. Following Hemingway's suggestion that looking at paintings can help a writer, Gaines has come to recognize the importance of selection and a well-placed item. He believes that viewing art helps him "describe a beautiful room with only two or three things, without having to go through everything in the room" (Lowe, 297). In short, he employs a visual economy to accompany his verbal restraint.

A less predictable source of inspiration, though one reiterating the same theme, has come from his appreciation of athletes. Although he has always recognized the value of discipline, Gaines pays particular homage to the discipline of athletes: "I know the discipline of athletes, and I know the same discipline must pertain to the writer, to the artist. He must be disciplined. He must do things over and over and over and over and over" (Lowe, 207). Inspired by the skill and grace of Muhammad Ali, Gaines has noted how Ali directs his blows "where they will have the greatest effect. Each one is calculated. . . . That's the kind of thing I would like to see in writing. If you are going to use words, put them where they are going to have the greatest and most lasting effect" (93). To approximate this effect, Gaines listens closely to speech and particularly to music.

Wherever he has lived, and despite the fact that he cannot carry a tune, Gaines has had music in his life: "Whether I'm playing jazz or classical music, or just the radio, I usually have music in the background, but soft, so it does not disturb me. I have to keep music. It relaxes me, and at the same time it gives me a sense of rhythm, of beat" (Lowe, 210). As readers might expect, Gaines has eclectic taste; his vast collection of recordings includes jazz, blues, spirituals, and classical music. More than providing rhythm, music has inspired story and mood. He has turned to blues singers for descriptions of black experience during the 1920s and 1930s, especially to Bessie Smith, Josh White, Ledbelly, and Lightnin' Hopkins. "The whites did the newspaper thing of the time, but when it came down to the more intimate things, I think the black blues singers gave us better descriptions than even the black writers did" (209). Gaines finds in jazz the same lessons he marks in athletic achievement: the importance of repetition and the role of musical understatement, playing around an idea instead of direct depiction for a more powerful effect.

Apparent indirection toward a very conscious goal seems a pattern in Gaines's career. From the earliest days of writing, he believed that work was not merely the physical act of writing. Work means "having your antennae out" (Lowe, 211), being tuned in to the life around you. And being a writer is not simply the act of observing others; it is, according to Gaines, *being*—absorbing the atmosphere you're in. He says he goes "back to Louisiana just to be" (211). Having struck a balance between being and thinking, Gaines does not consider himself an intellectual: "I am not an intellectual and don't want to be. An intellectual studies books, not people. I don't know if an intellectual knows how to drink at a bar, and they don't know how to act with people who are not intellectuals. They don't know how to talk with them" (146). Ultimately, Gaines is a writer who has found his own way, a writer impervious to fashion or commercial interests, a writer quite comfortable with who he is. And this brings us to yet another possible literary label.

Because of the importance of place in his work, Gaines has sometimes been called a southern writer. This is one literary label he doesn't categorically deny, though he points out that most of what he has written about the South has been composed in San Francisco. Still, he acknowledges, "I'm always in Louisiana even though I'm not living there" (Lowe, 152). Once again, however, Gaines does not fit into the most convenient southern literary category, Southern Gothic. Unlike such writers as Flannery O'Connor, Erskine Caldwell, or Lee Smith, Gaines does not exaggerate regional characteristics for comic effect or for their symbolic importance. His South plays a different role. More than background, Gaines's South often works like a character rather than setting. Weather, in particular, plays a key role—setting the mood, reflecting psychological states, forcing characters either inside, to reflect upon what they believe, or outside, to reconsider in another light. Though he employs the heat and humidity of late summer in *Of Love and Dust*, Gaines often employs dreary winter weather in "The Sky Is Gray," *In My Father's House*, and *A Lesson Before Dying*. More than many southern writers, Gaines exploits the subtext of his Louisiana setting, evoking history and the custom of caste and class. Thus, James and his mother in "The Sky Is Gray" know they cannot walk into any Bayonne store, they must go back of town to eat, and they avoid looking straight into the eyes of any white person. Directing readers' attention to dust, rain, season, or the acts of crossing a river or opening a gate, Gaines employs setting to its fullest extent. The land itself may be beautiful, its topographical features a part of the action. But beyond this, the setting has far-reaching thematic implications because it is weighed with human history.

Southern writers are often noted for their ability to tell elaborate stories. Lee Smith, Pat Conroy, and Alan Gurganus, for example, all tell good yarns, frequently at length, with emphasis on the sheer pleasure of language and its southern permutations. These often voluble writers depend upon episode to push their stories forward, moving their stories largely through character action. Gaines is often noted for his brilliant approximation of spoken language, but he doesn't believe that telling a story is the most important element of writing. From the beginning of his career, he has always valued fictional form over the plot's content. In other words, the details of a story take a decided second place to *how* the story is told. Gaines puts it this way: "We can go down the block right now and find a guy on the next corner who'll tell the biggest and truest story you can ever hear. Now, putting that story down on paper so that a million people can read, and feel, and hear it like you on that street corner, that's going to take form. That's *writing*" (Lowe, 114). Instead of expanding language, he pares it to a minimum, and instead of telling the same story a number of times, he moves from a number of directions. The result is a tightly woven fictional fabric instead of a loose, voluminous one.

In addition to being called a southern writer, Gaines may also fit into a category based on his thematic concerns. Drawing upon what is certainly the most pervasive theme in western literature, Gaines has his characters engage in a search for role, understanding, and significance in and of their world. This literary category based on theme is known as the *bildungsroman*, a German word roughly translated as "a novel of education or upbringing." One could refer to *The Odyssey* as the first such example, and the term can be applied to many other works as varied as *Moll Flanders* (1722), *Wilhelm Meister's Apprenticeship* (1795–1796), *Invisible Man* (1952), *Song of Solomon* (1977), and *The Prince of Tides* (1986). While this theme has been used in a great deal of formula fiction, in the hands of a literary artist it always assumes freshness and power. Virtually all of Gaines's protagonists, from the youngest child in "A Long Day in November" to Miss Jane Pittman, experience a series of "lessons" that teach them something about the value of life. During whatever fictional time allotted them, even a few hours as is the case of *A Gathering of Old Men*, they grow in understanding the world about them, and they learn about their place in the world. More than having his characters learn, Gaines wants his readers to learn something about themselves. As he says, "my aim in literature is to develop character so that if you pick up the book, you will see something you feel is true, something not seen before, that will develop your character from that day forward" (Lowe, 252).

Beyond these two categories, Gaines seems to belong most clearly to a long tradition of literary realists, a tradition that reaches back into the nineteenth century and continues today. Realism, like most literary terms, is defined in a number of ways and by a number of characteristics. It rejects sentimentality and speculative idealism in an attempt to render something approaching an authentic texture of reality. Thus, characters use ungrammatical language, they often live in humble circumstances that are not picturesque, and the conflicts of their lives are not neatly resolved so that they "live happily ever after." Indeed, realism tends to depict things as they are, not as readers would wish them to be. A review of the list of writers who have most influenced Ernest Gaines is, in fact, a long list of realists, beginning with Turgenev and Twain and continuing through Hemingway. Gaines's realistic ethic is best expressed in simple terms: he describes himself as "a writer who happens to draw from his environment what his life is, what heritage is" (Lowe, 229). This heritage includes poverty, racism, political abuse, physical violence, self-deceit, and self-doubt, as well as love, duty, commitment, and honor, humor, and beauty. Trying to render an accurate reflection of the feelings of both black and white residents of rural Louisiana, he says, "I don't romanticize it at all" (124).

For forty years, Ernest Gaines has worked to write well and to tell the truth, actions that require, beyond talent, considerable moral courage and physical stamina. No one knows this better than Gaines: "Writing is a very difficult thing and writing well is more difficult. The only moral obligation the writer has is to write well and never do any work that he cannot feel proud of. He owes that to his art and not to anyone else but to that work . . . not to an audience . . . not to himself" (Lowe, 251). Rather than lapse into self-imitation, Gaines has worked not to repeat himself. The result is a body of work unique in its personally created world. Beyond any literary category, Ernest Gaines will be remembered for the Quarters. Drawn from experience with the texture of reality, this literary place assumes a mythic quality similar to Faulkner's Yoknopatawpha County or Sherwood Anderson's Winesburg, Ohio. Gaines not only created and populated this world, he has made it representative of all worlds: "I've always felt that the artist writes the whole, he writes big—I don't think he knows the little small things, because he sees the large thing, and he puts that down" (309). This large view presented in a small Louisiana place assumes a mythic quality assuring its permanence in American literature.

3

Catherine Carmier
(1964)

When he was sixteen years old, Ernest Gaines, homesick for Point Cou-pee, sat down in Vallejo and began to write his first novel. By his own admission, he did not know what he was doing. But he began with an image of a river as a barrier between the races and went on from there. Recalling a light-skinned girl named Catherine and his childhood attrac-tion to her, Gaines wrote a simple love story between a fair young woman and a dark young man. When his manuscript was returned from a New York City publisher, Gaines destroyed it. However, he never quite forgot the outline of his tale. It remained with him through college and his creative writing program at Stanford, where he was told by a visiting publisher that he couldn't make money writing short stories. Gaines then decided to write a novel. Casting about for ideas, he recalled his original story, and five years later, this story became *Catherine Carmier*.

Like many novels, *Catherine Carmier* is about change and its effects. It is a young man's novel asking questions of place and purpose that young people in particular wrestle with: Why aren't things the way they were? What am I going to do with my life? Where is my life? Should I feel guilty for rejecting the truths of those I love? This novel goes further—much further—than the personal, however. It looks at culture, seemingly protected from the changes transforming the United States in the 1960s, and dissects its economic and social hierarchy.

After a ten-year absence from his home in south Louisiana, Jackson

Bradley returns to the plantation where he was raised by his great aunt Charlotte. He had left Louisiana to join his parents in California and has recently graduated from college there. The time is the early 1960s, when the Civil Rights Movement in the United States is gathering momentum. Jackson encounters his childhood friends; Catherine Carmier, the Creole daughter of Raoul and Della Carmier; and Brother, his closest male friend. Stepping off the bus, Jackson at first fails to notice many differences, but in the coming weeks of his visit he will slowly recognize the limits of tradition. Change has transformed Jackson physically from boyhood to manhood, and it has also transformed the plantation's landscape, with more and more land being farmed by the Cajuns, thus changing the economic fortunes of black residents who have tried to make a living off the land. Some readers may not understand the agricultural practice known as sharecropping. This system was instituted after slavery, when white landowners parceled out their property for farming to a variety of farmers, both white and black, on "shares," or percentages of crop harvest. Since the landowner usually controlled not only the land but also housing, seeds, machinery, farm implements, work animals, and often food supplies, and since the poorest people generally engaged in sharecropping, only landowners could profit. It was a system that ensured—at best—subsistence for those who worked the land. Reflecting a hierarchy of value based on skin color, sharecropping often portioned off the least productive land to black farmers, ensuring their continuing poverty.

Shortly after exiting the bus, Jackson notes changes in the landscape as Cajuns and mechanization have turned farming into a business, replacing what he remembers as a slower moving, pastoral way of life. Bud Grover, the plantation owner, has given more and more land to the Cajuns to farm, dispossessing black farmers, many of whom have left for jobs in Baton Rouge and New Orleans. Gaines uses the competition among the various social castes of Louisiana culture to dramatize the strains of social change that seem to surround but have not yet come to this area, and he employs the particular cultural nuances of south Louisiana, with its four-tiered system. The people on the plantation claim different cultural heritages. Bud Grover, the owner, is white, European descended, with some claim to English descent. Beneath him are the Cajuns, also white people, but of French descent, emigrating from Nova Scotia in the 1700s. Having called Nova Scotia "the New Acadia," and themselves "Acadians," the word became shortened to "Cajuns." "Creole" is a term to suggest a mixed cultural heritage, and in Louisiana, distinctions may be made between Creoles of Spanish, French, and Italian descent and those who may also come from Africa. Gaines's use of "Creole" generally focuses on people of mixed heritage, with some link to Africa. This class, represented in *Catherine Carmier* by Raoul Carmier and his family, served as a social buffer between European-descended whites and African-descended blacks. Neither black nor white, many of these very light-skinned people made their own culture in the past, enjoying more privileges than their darker kin but not the full civil rights of their white relatives. But with social barriers eroding over time, the Creoles (of color) now stand alone, as isolated as Raoul Carmier and his family.

POINT OF VIEW

Catherine Carmier demonstrates many of the difficulties of first novels and shows the promise of its author. Gaines chose to write this novel in third-person omniscient, often shifting into an approximation of first-person as he moves among his characters. But Gaines hasn't yet developed full control, so there are instances of editorializing, of the author's intrusion into the text, to make sure that readers will fully know what his characters are thinking and feeling. Third-person omniscient can be quite effective because it allows the author to know what every character feels, thinks, and says. But Gaines also shows the influence of Ernest Hemingway, who perfected third-person dramatic, recording dialogue and gesture as if he were a camera. Because this narrative perspective is so objective, readers must draw their own conclusions. At this point in his career, Gaines had not yet found a balance between omniscience and dramatic rendering. The result in *Catherine Carmier* is an occasionally awkward joining of the two points of view, sometimes telling the reader precisely what to think and sometimes leaving the readers to draw their own conclusions. Gaines's characters frequently need to convey a sense of paradox and uncertainty, but because he cannot trust his characters to accurately dramatize this, he adds to the text, piling up questions and contradictions instead of paring them down and using only gesture and implication. Though he uses gesture, especially eye contact, he also tells his readers what the gestures say, and this can at times lead to writing that Gaines himself would now find somewhat absurd. At one point, as Catherine and Jackson gaze upon each other, they share the following: "Then a little smile came on her mouth. It seemed to say—All right, nothing can come of our love, but we can like each other, can't we? They can keep us apart but they can't make us stop liking each other, can they?" (125).

Of course, this awkwardness is entirely unintentional. It indicates a writer still finding his own way. At this point, Gaines was still very much under the influence of writers like William Faulkner, Ernest Hemingway, and Ivan Turgenev. Gaines chose to model his first novel on Turgenev's *Fathers and Sons*, whose structure, point of view, and plot line are repeated in *Catherine Carmier*. But having also come under the influence of Ernest Hemingway, with his use of simple sentences, repetitions, gesture, exploitation of silence and subtext, and sense of irony, Gaines cannot fulfill his ambitions. The result is a distance and lack of character development that cannot dramatically support his demanding thematic needs.

Jackson feels distant—as if he's moving in a familiar yet strange landscape. Now twenty-two, he consistently checks his reactions—part of him recalling a sense of connection to the plantation and the people who have known him, especially Aunt Charlotte; and part of him rejecting a place where black people continue to be at the bottom of a social and economic scale, where there are few opportunities and skin color plays such a major role in dividing one member of the community from another. Because he has been gone for ten years and because he is college educated, he sees his home from a different perspective. It seems frozen in its old ways. At the same time, his experience in California has taught Jackson that while the forms of discrimination in Louisiana are open— if often unspoken—the same forms persist in California, where they are less direct. Jackson is looking for a place and a purpose, though he agrees with Madame Bayonne's use of "dignity" and "truth" (81) as the objects of his search. In Louisiana, he can find neither. But at the same time, he recognizes that he won't find them in California, either.

Catherine, like Jackson, is also estranged from her community, though for different reasons. Skin color has kept her separate from both white and black communities. Like her father and mother, Catherine is very light skinned, and because she will not be accepted by the white community, and her father opposes her relationship with anyone out of their extremely small Creole class, Catherine literally has no place other than the farm where she has grown to maturity. Still, she shares impulses with all young adults, desiring to find her own life while firmly tied into her parents' relationship. Catherine, like Jackson, is full of contradictory desires.

Gaines attempts to give us insights into the minds of many of his characters in this novel, a technique he will perfect in *The Autobiography of Miss Jane Pittman*. But in *Catherine Carmier* he never establishes complete control, trying to maintain authorial distance and simultaneously bringing his characters' hopes, desires, questions, and insecurities to his readers. While Gaines works hard to give his main characters individual voices, Jackson and Catherine actually speak in similar cadences and tones, with very few contrasting grammatical markers. The result is intermittent immediacy. When some of his characters speak, it is with authentic sounding approximations of colloquial language. At other times, the language will be quite formal, moving readers to the periphery of the action. The result is a distance between character and reader and some confusion as to the source of their inaction.

PLOT DEVELOPMENT AND STRUCTURE

There is little movement in this novel, all of the action taking place within a month. Elements precipitating action, however, lie in the region's and characters' past. Divided into three parts, *Catherine Carmier* moves in a linear progression, from Jackson's arrival to his climactic fight with Raoul. Part One focuses on Jackson's return, setting up the racial and economic tensions of the novel, especially through the comments of Lillian, Catherine's sister, who maintains that Raoul's world is dead, and Jackson, who concludes this section by rejecting the submissive religious notions he has been taught as "bourgeois farce" (100). This section ends with an image of death, as Jackson notes the effect of drought on the bean crop.

Part Two involves the painful wavering of both Jackson and Catherine as they struggle with their feelings for one another. Torn by loyalty to those who have raised them, they nevertheless manage to leave the plantation for brief periods. Away from the plantation, they can be intimate in a way that neither feels when at home. Jackson strives to find a way to tell his Aunt Charlotte that he doesn't plan to remain on the plantation while she maintains hope that Jackson will return to the church. Instead of discussing their perspectives, both Jackson and Charlotte avoid conversation—even physical contact. Jackson also contends with feelings of emptiness, wanting to feel something. When he looks at the church/ school building at the end of this section, Jackson still lacks a sense of resolution and direction.

In Part Three, Raoul Carmier admits that he made a "mistake" in sending Lillian away to be educated by his family, but this does not mean he has abandoned his belief in caste distinctions. Indeed, in his climactic fist fight with Jackson, Raoul imagines that Jackson is Marky, Della's son by her former lover, and his intensity suggests his level of desperation to maintain a *status quo*. While the male characters engage in the action, the female characters set it in motion. Lillian arranges for Jackson to meet Catherine, and Gaines gives Della the final word, telling Jackson that Catherine will eventually join him. This ending, however, is ambiguous, suggesting a union of Jackson and Catherine only as a possibility. Gaines has stated in subsequent interviews that Catherine "couldn't exist outside of the South" (Lowe, 32), denying this textual possibility. Regardless of the novel's ambiguities, *Catherine Carmier* is imbued with a sense of fatality, its characters terminating in counterbalance. In the end, Jackson, who signals change, stands at the Carmier house waiting for Catherine who "never comes" (248).

From the very outset of his career, Gaines has expressed a belief in form. Again and again he has stressed a novel's structure over imaginative narrative. Certainly we see evidence of this in *Catherine Carmier*, which seems almost classical in its clean and simple structure. The few critics who have commented on this novel, however, note a certain imbalance between Jackson Bradley, the main character, and Catherine, the title character who plays only a supportive if highly significant role. Of course, Catherine represents important issues to her lover and father, but she carries little textual weight. This difficulty seems more a result of a novelist in the making than a thematic problem. Gaines has stated that initially the novel tended to focus more on the Carmier family and Catherine than on Jackson, and that her name became his title more out of a last minute decision than as a result of deliberation. (Lowe, 32).

CHARACTER DEVELOPMENT

Dialogue helps readers see and know characters. As many professional writers will say, dialogue *is* character. Jackson Bradley seems particularly tongue-tied during his visit, literally having nothing to say to most of the characters except for "How've you been?" (123). Much of this inability to speak derives from his confusion, and is thus a major means of conveying character. His return to Louisiana is literally and figuratively a crossroads, as he compares one region and all it represents to an unknown future. Setting his novel in the early sixties, with the Civil Rights Movement gaining momentum throughout the South, Gaines suggests a general state of flux. His references to Freedom Riders (black riders who affirmed their civil rights by refusing to sit in the back of the bus on interstate routes) implies that change is coming—even to this remote area of Louisiana, where traditions die slowly. Thus, Jackson notes changes in landscape, hears that the Cajuns have almost complete control over the farmland, and sees few opportunities for his contemporaries. Knowing that he will be held accountable for his language and knowing that what he says may be hurtful to people he cares about, he relies on silence.

Gaines gives us a profound sense of a character who is "empty," (191) unable to feel a deep sense of connection to anyone or anything. Though modeled on Bazarov of *Fathers and Sons*, Jackson is not quite a nihilist, someone who believes in nothing. Although he has abandoned Aunt Charlotte's religious convictions and lost faith in the myth of the North as a place where African Americans can be treated as equals, Jackson clearly wants to believe in something. Ironically, Jackson may represent change, as the Cajuns fear, but he never actually states his position. He talks to few characters, holding his lengthiest conversations with his former teacher, Madame Bayonne—conversations we are told focus on social and political changes but which we do not often hear. The result is reader speculation resting on very little firsthand evidence.

Aunt Charlotte represents the past, and here Gaines's ability shows to better advantage. A devout woman whose life has conformed to her community, Aunt Charlotte has lived for Jackson, pinning all of her hopes on her great nephew, dreaming of his return which will reflect favorably on their family. Gaines will often have a character designated by the community as "the One," usually a male character selected and groomed to become a leader. Though there is little evidence that the community has selected Jackson, there is no doubt that Charlotte has decided in his absence that Jackson will become the center of her community. Certainly, Charlotte affirms that he is the center of her life. Jackson, however, has decided not to remain in Louisiana even before he leaves California, but he cannot muster the courage to disappoint a woman he loves. And though she probably suspects the truth, Charlotte clings to her hope that Jackson will stay to teach school. These two characters, living in a small house, consciously time their exits and entrances to avoid discussion of what the other suspects. Charlotte's character is profoundly conservative, valuing a continuation of the *status quo* rather than inviting change. The four-year-old calendar she places in Jackson's room depicting Christ kneeling in the garden of Gethsemane summarizes her belief in submission to a higher power. Charlotte cannot challenge authority. Thus, she is alarmed when she momentarily believes that Jackson might be bringing a white woman home, and she is equally upset about Jackson's love for Catherine. Like Raoul, she respects the caste system and works to perpetuate it.

Equally conservative is Raoul Carmier, a man whose social position is evaporating before him. Neither black nor white, Raoul is literally working himself to death on land he loves and simultaneously trying to retain his status based on color. The last remaining farmer who isn't a Cajun, he has continued working the land at the expense of his family, from whom he is almost entirely estranged. Raoul scorns his wife and sisters, though they are the only acceptable company he can keep. He claims to love only Catherine, having emotionally abandoned his wife Della more than twenty years in the past. The tortured story of Della's love affair with a dark-skinned man, the son from their relationship, the son's death which is blamed on Raoul, and the disappearance of Della's lover provide a formidable backdrop and constant warning to the black community. They should stay away from Raoul's family. The community believes that Raoul has made Catherine his "wife," noting his devotion to her and his jealousy of any suitors. What becomes increasingly clear is that Raoul is fighting a losing battle. He cannot compete with the Cajuns' tractors, which allow them to efficiently farm more (and more productive) land, just as he cannot continue to compete with Catherine's young suitors. Gaines has Raoul's character equate Catherine to the land, so that in losing one, he appears to lose the other. In this complex equation resides one of the most delicate of Gaines's thematic concerns dealing with intraracial prejudice. While Raoul's reasons for maintaining a separate and exclusive status are clearly racist, his Creole status is the source of personal pride which forms the basis of his courage, determination, and tenacity, which are admirable. This fine distinction is pointed out to readers through Catherine and Della, whose love and admiration for Raoul remain constant, despite his obsessive behavior. Raoul's climactic fight with Jackson shows a desperate move to prevent change, for in doing so, he is battling to maintain a clearly obsolete social system. But in fighting Jackson, Raoul also struggles to maintain what he knows to be the most admirable part of his character.

Catherine's character is similar to Jackson's in that she doesn't tell us much about herself. We know from her actions that she sees herself as a buffer between her estranged parents and between her sister Lillian and her parents. This latter rupture has occurred after Raoul's family insisted on raising Lillian as a Creole, having first assured themselves of her color. Taken away from her immediate family, Lillian has been taught to "hate black" (48) and to despise her mother for having violated the strict caste system. Unlike Lillian, who has already told Catherine that she plans to go north and pass for white, Catherine feels a deep if sometimes contradictory connection to her parents, the land, and even the black community. Even as a child, she has not fully accepted her father's racist ideas. Though forbidden, she had made Jackson a guest in her house when they were children, and she shows few compunctions about resuming their friendship after his return. Indeed, she makes opportunities to have contact as their passions grow. Moreover, Catherine flouts Raoul's authority by borrowing his car so that she and Jackson can escape the plantation and their families' restrictive attitudes. Perhaps the most significant sign of Catherine's rebellion from her father's beliefs is her son Nelson. Her rejection of hatred suggests her largeness of spirit. Loving her parents and knowing their need for her presence, Catherine realizes that she cannot remain with Raoul and Della indefinitely, though she admires her father's determination so much that she refuses to abandon him. We see a degree of loyalty in her character, a loyalty others rely upon and that binds her to some practices in which she clearly doesn't believe, namely status based on color. Above all, Catherine wants people to care for each other, but she never directly expresses personal desires.

Since she is the title character, we tend to look closely at Catherine, for she suggests the thematic and narrative center of this novel. Gaines clearly wants us to admire Catherine, who has not succumbed to Raoul's racist attitudes. Even as a child, Catherine has moved easily among both Creoles and blacks, cultivating friendships at a distance. Partly this is self-protective, since she doesn't want to anger her father. But in protecting Raoul, in ensuring his devotion, is she self-destructive? Does she perpetuate a caste system in which she doesn't believe? Is she in danger of remaining her father's child though she is a grown woman? Lillian, who clearly believes the time has come for her sister to have her own life, encourages Jackson's attentions because she wants to undermine Raoul's seeming control of Catherine. And Catherine clearly plans to leave with Jackson as she steps over the threshold of her parents' home with Nelson in her arms. Only her father's knocking her aside stops her until Jackson shows signs of fighting Raoul. And in his inevitable defeat,

Raoul relinquishes Catherine, telling her to go with Jackson. Then, she refuses: "It's not over with, Daddy. You have stood this long. You can keep on standing. I'll stand beside you" (244). Her language tells readers that Raoul stands for more than maintaining attitudes; he inspires his daughter's loyalty because of his pride.

Gaines invests yet another female character with an important role in this novel. Madame Bayonne, Jackson's former teacher, seems to possess almost omniscient knowledge about plantation people and events. Named for the nearby town, a town that will come to occupy a central position in Gaines's fiction, Madame Bayonne tells both Jackson and readers almost everything we know about Raoul. She not only has insight into his relationship with Della and Catherine, she also recognizes the socioeconomic ramifications of Raoul's Creole status. Moreover, she is unequivocal in pointing out the responsibility of white men. Able to read characters at a glance, Madame Bayonne possesses an understanding so formidable that many characters avoid talking to her. With her almost comprehensive grasp of both her community and the larger world outside, Madame Bayonne offers Jackson an alternative means of dealing with the realities he encounters, in other words a means of living within a confining system without surrendering himself to it (Byerman, 69). He might come to occupy, as she does, a central place within the community, even while maintaining a distance. Readers might note how Gaines suggests Madame Bayonne's detachment by looking closely at her house, separated from others by a wall of flowers and shrubs.

THEMATIC CONCERNS

This brings us to the thematic heart of *Catherine Carmier*, for while Gaines may not have full control of point of view, he may be too much under the shadow of Hemingway, and though his characterization sometimes seems thin and his control heavy handed, his thematic development is extremely complex. With his opening scene in *Catherine Carmier*, Gaines gives readers a deep sense of social stratification, with Brother entering a store/post office and accepting as a matter of course the rude behavior of Claude, the white man behind the counter. The Cajuns outside have shared in the rudeness, attributing it to heat, but Brother must endure a sweeping kind of anger, one directed not so much at him as an individual but at an entire class of resident. Claude looks at Brother, swears, and says, "Why the hell can't y'all come out here the same time.

Look like the hotter it get the more you niggers want to bother people"
(3–4). This scene efficiently establishes a number of issues Gaines will
weave into his narrative: racial stratification and its effects upon his characters, regional economic issues, and attitudes toward social change.

Racial stratification is never simple, and Gaines does not treat this
issue in only black and white terms because racial mixing is such a significant part of Louisiana heritage. Nineteenth-century America was a
rich stew of nationalities which were often termed "races." Thus, the
Irish were considered an inferior "race" by the English, and Mediterra-
nean people such as Italians also occupied a position in a racial hierarchy
which involved virtually everyone—willingly or not. Because the population of south Louisiana was so diverse—already inhabited by Native
Americans, it was explored, claimed, and settled by both Spanish and
French before its purchase by the United States from France attracted
the Acadians and other nationalities—a good deal of mixing went on.
The presence of Africans merely increased the possibilities. Miscegena-
tion, the mixing of races, was, in fact, commonplace in the American
South, often occurring when white property owners raped or simply
appropriated black women for sexual purposes. The children of these
relationships were deemed "black" because in a legal anomaly practiced
only in the United States, children of slave women followed the "condition of the mothers." Everywhere else, of course, children belonged to
their fathers. Children of interracial relationships did, too, only more
literally than other children. They were the legal property of their fathers.
Sometimes, though, relationships between owner and slave were based
on love, with white fathers freeing their children and giving them property. This class grew and became known as "free people of color," or
Creoles.

In a culture placing such value on skin color and parentage, everyone
is bound to be affected. When Gaines injects the story of how the Carmiers came to inhabit the large house of the white overseer, it is to per-
sonalize what has happened and emphasize its meaning. Robert
Carmier, Raoul's father, asks Mack Grover for the house. "What color
are you?" Mack asks, and Robert claims that he is "colored" (8). Mack
offers another, presumably smaller, house, and Robert engages in a
standoff: "He had come up there as a man would come up to a man,
and he had asked for the house as a man should ask for a house" (9).
Robert, in fact, engages Mack as an equal, not as a subservient, as the
emphasis on the word "man" suggests. Because he is dealing with the
"best" of the Grovers, meaning the one most tolerant in his racial views,

Robert gets the house and selects the moving date. But all residents of the plantation do not share Grover's views, as two subsequent acts dramatize.

Robert's belief that he is equal to a white man plays a role in his decision to separate himself from the black community. If he cannot be white, he refuses to be "black," determined not to accept the inferior status it carries in the South. Thus, he separates himself from the entire black community from the very beginning. On moving day, when the bridge to the house breaks, Robert refuses help from the black community, using only family members to haul furniture. His insistence upon his family's separation is reinforced by two subsequent images that will play a role throughout this novel: the trees and shrubbery isolating the Carmier house and the gates that must be opened and closed when any family member enters or exits the property. These physical barriers alert Robert's immediate neighbors to stay away, and indeed there are almost no uninvited guests at the Carmier home. Robert's actions, however, are self-defeating, just as they are in the wider community, because in rebuffing assistance, he becomes an easy target for the Cajuns, who look upon Robert as their most threatening competition.

When Robert beats a Cajun to the cane derrick, he disproves the widespread belief that all white men are superior to all black men. Indeed, Robert's sense of competitiveness publicly illustrates what the men of the quarters privately admit: that he is a very capable man. But since black people keep Cajuns from the bottom of the social scale, Cajuns cannot publicly recognize equality. Thus, the Cajun reacts violently when Robert insists that he "come in front" (13), again establishing equal ground. Since the Cajun doesn't operate that way, he works secretively to murder Robert. Robert's "disappearance" and the hasty move by his survivors out of the big house suggests the terrorist tactics of the Ku Klux Klan and other organizations that worked to maintain a subservient status for African Americans. There is no investigation, suggesting official collusion and reinforcing the belief that black claims to equality, of whatever shade, will result in death.

Raoul inherits his father's position, standing apart and working very hard to assert a manhood that will be denied him, not for what he can do but for what others perceive him to be. As in his father's case, the separation that Raoul insists upon changes no attitudes; it isolates him. Obsessed with proving his manhood, he becomes self-defeating. Alone, he tries to make his farm as productive as the Cajuns'. This obsession becomes a repetition of the John Henry story, pitting man against machine. Raoul has almost become an automaton, a human machine, working from light to light in a losing contest, driven by pride to prove his ability in a culture that will judge by skin color first. More importantly, as subsequent novels by Gaines will dramatize, Raoul's inability to see any value in the black community will escalate his defeat. Raoul's claim to racial superiority mirrors that of the white community, and in so doing suggests not merely the internalization of white values but their self-destructive capability. What Gaines will do in all of his work is to insist on "the democracy of color among African-Americans" (Griffin, 44).

The black community shows a willingness to accept the Carmiers, despite their solitariness. Aunt Charlotte's disapproval of Jackson's relationship with Catherine seems to rise more from her fear of Raoul's reaction than a sense of social separation. Just as the white community punishes sexual transgressions with lynching, Raoul has apparently murdered Della's lover, and Charlotte rightly fears further violence. But this nevertheless serves to reinforce a belief in a social hierarchy. Unwilling to analyze the end results of continuing to make social and racial distinctions, she is fearful of change.

Racial stratification is a part of southern economics, rising as it does from slavery. For labor intensive crops such as rice, sugarcane, and cotton, large human work forces were needed, but machines developed to supplant or increase human efficiency make substantial work forces obsolete. Still, for a long time after the Civil War, the southern agricultural economy remained dependent upon a large, low-wage labor force. The people, already in place, developed into communities that reflected much the same values as they had during slavery. Gaines's novels will often direct reader attention to social changes that occur in the wake of mechanization, charting the death of a way of life that had its own rich beauty despite its economic poverty. With tractors making the Cajun farmers more productive, black farmers are literally dispossessed of the only way of life they have known. Worse, they are forced to leave their families for work in urban areas. This, in turn, depletes the rural community of its youth, the old people remaining much as the novel suggests. The way of life that in part draws Jackson home is dying, and along with it the traditions of communal values that allowed people to survive.

Gaines is not sentimental about an economic system that perpetuates poverty for a large segment of people. But he does paint a landscape in which shared labor created strong human bonds, a sense of communal responsibility, such as we see in Mary Louise's caring for Aunt Charlotte and Brother's voluntary collection of welfare checks. As rural jobs disappear, so will successive generations, depleting the communities of their vigor until they quite literally die, and with them the intimate understanding that comes with sharing a common heritage. More significant, though, is the perpetual issue of human value in the face of technology. What happens to humans and human values when confronted with unfeeling efficiency?

With the economy changing and the accompanying population shifts, the characters of *Catherine Carmier* are forced to confront their own attitudes toward social change. Much of this is done indirectly, since there is considerable resistance to any acknowledgement of civil rights activities. The Cajuns speculate on whether Jackson might be one of "them demonstrate people" (7), and Brother is cautiously evasive for good reason. But the novel's focus rests on the Carmier house and its inhabitants. When Lillian first arrives, she asks Catherine "what's wrong" with their house (46), and continues by exclaiming over her education in hating because they derive from the same cause: discrimination on the basis of color. Lillian's plan to "pass" for white shows a recognition of the passing of Creole status, but it nevertheless remains a part of racial distinctions. She aligns herself with Raoul, Charlotte, and Raoul's sisters in continuing to make distinctions.

Jackson and Catherine, on the other hand, move more easily among all groups. In fact, when they are off the plantation, they are quite easy with one another, suggesting it's the continuation of obsolete attitudes that restricts their language—and love. This freedom, as Jackson knows, is relative, and it is not limited to the South. Wherever he goes, Jackson seeks "dignity" and "truth," but he has recognized that he's not alone in this quest, that all races are seeking the same goal.

In writing about a common human struggle for truth and dignity, Ernest Gaines stands apart from many African American writers of his generation such as John A. Williams, James Baldwin, and John O. Killens, who generally focused their works of the 1950s and 1960s on the "terrors and hopes" of being a young black male in America (Baker, 16). These fears increased to a literary militancy that Gaines's fiction includes but does not emphasize. Instead, his fiction will come much closer to the ordinary reality of human existence by expressing a variety of attitudes toward social change. The two educated characters of *Catherine Carmier*, Jackson and Madame Bayonne, clearly grasp the inevitable if slow onset of change. Madame Bayonne tells Jackson that she can remain on the plantation as long as she "keeps her nose clean" (78), suggesting how well she understands the role of silence in maintaining the attitudes of the past. The characters' preference for living with secrets rather than acknowledging truth plays a significant role in this novel and is an insightful comment on human resistence to change. Unlike his contemporaries, who largely condemned those who resisted social change, Gaines shows remarkable understanding and sympathy to characters fearful of and knowledgeable about the often violent consequences of altering the *status quo*. His fictional treatment is marked by nuance and ambiguity instead of militant rhetoric and violence. By embracing all the races, Gaines distinguishes himself from his contemporaries, who largely depict America in stark black and white terms. Recognizing the complexity of racism and its insidious effects upon everyone, Gaines's rendering of his ideas brought him criticism which he largely ignored in favor of his own artistic vision.

A FEMINIST READING

It's very unlikely that Ernest Gaines was writing for a literary critic when he wrote *Catherine Carmier*, and he certainly was not writing with a feminist critic in mind. Like most theoretical approaches, feminist criticism can be both complex and difficult to define. What follows is a brief history and working definition. Some feminist critics trace its beginning as a critical approach to Virginia Woolf's *A Room of One's Own* (1919). Woolf points out that men, who control political, economic, social, and literary institutions, define what it means to be female. But great minds, she maintained, share both male and female characteristics. A female literary genius, Woolf maintained, would be possible if women writers had not only financial resources and a room of their own but also teachers, scholars, and critics to show the way (Bressler, 104). Simone de Beauvoir's *The Second Sex* (1949) is often held to be another important text in feminist criticism. Beginning with the premise that French culture and, in fact, all western cultures are patriarchal, Beauvoir reiterated Woolf's observation that males get to define the female. But she went further, pointing out that because they get to define the meaning of women, men see women as Other and thus hardly see women at all. Women, then, become nonexistent in cultural institutions, including religion, government, and education. Beauvoir went on to encourage women to define themselves, to become significant human beings in their own right (104).

Ultimately, feminist criticism would draw upon both texts and develop three differing strains—French, American, and British—each reflecting the intellectual training of the academic system.

While French feminists primarily concentrate on the exploration of language as it reflects and influences the way we think about ourselves and our world, American feminists tend to focus largely on such textual issues as voice, tone, and theme. British feminist critics often find the American approach too text bound. Their approach tends to pay more attention to political and historical details. They want to place texts within the historical conditions that create them. Thus, their critical approach features an interest in historical process as it promotes social change. Because of his recreation of a unified society within a particular time frame, because he often focuses on the theme of change as it affects all aspects of life, and because he often features female characters, Gaines's work lends itself more to a British theoretical approach than an American one, and less so to a French one. But adding an American theoretical perspective to the British one can only add to the richness of a discussion.

We can begin with Gaines's use of female characters and the attitudes expressed by and through them. In selecting Catherine as his title character, Gaines—however accidentally—throws readers' focus on a remarkably passive character. Admired throughout the community for her beauty and her kindness, Catherine seems bound to the traditions that limit both her role and place. She appears to have little independent sense of Self, contented to remain with her parents, though she is twenty-two years old and the mother of a two-year-old son. In this respect, she represents the middle-class values of her parents and the larger society of the early 1960s. Were it not for the living reminder of Nelson, readers might accept her as a conventional female character. But Catherine's sexual maturity and her rebellion from middle-class sexual values are explicit in her son.

Catherine finds herself in a dying world, one in which she serves both supporting and symbolic roles. To Raoul she is a reminder of his life before his love for Della mutated. She is more his child than her mother's. Indeed, he gives her the "easier" housework while Della works alongside him (like a man) in the field. And to Jackson, Catherine becomes a "light," a symbolic guide for his lost soul. That both men see her in stereotypical and dependent terms says much about their time and society. Catherine wears a pink dress selected and purchased for her by Raoul, the color and style suggesting both her immature dependence on him and his gender stereotyping. Later in the novel, Jackson, trying to decide on a gift for Catherine, determines a doll as an appropriate token of his love. Both dress and doll underscore male notions of female immaturity. Further, both Raoul and Jackson assert possession of Catherine, as if she were chattel, with the winner of their climactic fight claiming her as a prize. When Gaines has Della call Jackson the "hero," he emphasizes a belief in male privilege.

This kind of stereotypical and conventional treatment of female character is undercut, however, by their rebellion. All of the Carmier women, seemingly submissive and passive, determine their lives. Della has chosen to remain with Raoul out of love instead of economic dependence, as she makes clear to Jackson at the end of the novel. Her extramarital love affair with a dark-skinned man suggests a woman capable of flouting convention. Della may conform to Raoul's commands that she separate herself from the black community, and she may accept his punishment of her infidelity, but her presence also serves as a continual reminder of Raoul's deficiencies as a man and father.

Lillian has also determined her future. Though she has been a hostage to Raoul's racist attitudes, raised by his family in New Orleans, she has already seen that the Creole world is obsolete, though not before internalizing its values. Thus, she finds herself actively hating the black community and suspicious of the white. Her character reflects the damage that racist values inflict, but she is redeemed by her candor. More than any other character in *Catherine Carmier*, Lillian expresses her views and is active in promoting her agenda, especially in trying to separate Catherine from her parents. The text insists, perhaps too much, upon Lillian's "sincerity." But the repetition of this word also implies that Lillian acts not merely in her own interest. Lillian therefore becomes not merely a supporting figure in this novel but one to be examined very closely.

While Gaines may use female characters in fairly stereotypical ways, he nevertheless imbues them with strength and integrity, characteristics relatively atypical of fictional females of the early 1960s. Jackson and Raoul's limiting ideas of the roles women play in their lives accurately reflects the patriarchy of the South and its effects upon the whole, for these male characters know all too well their place and the personal effects of social hierarchy. Members of the white power structure, suggested by characters racing a speed boat up and down the river merely for entertainment and by the drunken figure of Bud Grover, seem oblivious to the struggles for survival of those beneath them. But the creator of *Catherine Carmier* remains sympathetic to the whole of the community. Instead of a polemic message, Gaines leaves readers with a profound sense of loss, not because of lost innocence but because of lost opportunities. In this respect, he stands above many of his peers.

4

Of Love and Dust
(1967)

In recalling the impetus behind *Of Love and Dust*, Ernest Gaines says that in order to get his collection of stories (*Bloodline*) published, he was advised he would have to produce a second novel (Lowe, 318). He started by taking the character of Proctor Lewis from "Three Men" in *Bloodline* and dressing him in silk shirts and brown and white shoes. Then, a number of memories merged to form the character and situation of Marcus Payne, *Of Love and Dust*'s defiant protagonist. Thinking not only of Lewis but also Muhammad Ali and a friend who had killed a man in a knife fight, Gaines also recalled a Lightnin' Hopkins tune, "Mr. Tim Moore's Farm." In this narrative blues piece, a black man laments his move to a place so bad even "the overseer would never stand and grin: 'you keep out of the jailhouse, nigger; I'll keep you out [of] the pen' " (100). Gaines imaginatively bonded out his friend (who served time in Angola Prison) and placed him on a plantation. Knowing that his character would need to cause a considerable disturbance, Gaines simply reversed the widely accepted plantation practice of white overseers' having sexual relations with black women. Given this direction, he found *Of Love and Dust* to be "the easiest [book] to write" (319).

This novel continues Gaines's favorite themes, including the unequal distribution of wealth, race and caste, and the conflict between the past and change. Marcus Payne, awaiting trial for killing a man in a knife fight, is "bonded out" to plantation owner Marshall Hebert. Defiant from the outset, Marcus recognizes the practice as another form of slavery and announces his intentions to escape after his trial. Meanwhile, he is put to work in the fields and harrassed by Sidney Bonbon, the white overseer who attempts to break his spirit. Marcus believes himself to be equal— if not superior—to Bonbon, an uneducated Cajun. To prove this to himself, he attempts to seduce Pauline Guerin, Bonbon's longtime mistress and love.

But when Pauline rebuffs his attempts, Marcus determines an alternate means of illustrating his manhood. He turns to Bonbon's neglected white wife, Louise. This act is the ultimate violation of race codes, which freely allowed white men sexual liaisons with black women but sentenced any black man to death for having been accused of sexual transgression (imagined or real) with a white woman. Marcus's actions threaten plantation order. Only the narrator, Jim Kelly, seems to grow into understanding the delicate situation before him and what really motivates Marcus. If white culture denies him status as a worker, Marcus will demonstrate his masculine superiority through his seduction of his tormentors' women.

POINT OF VIEW

For his second novel, Gaines chose a first-person narrator, thirty-three-year-old Jim Kelly. He says that the story needed "a guy who could communicate with different sides, with the most conservative as well as the most militant. And . . . he must be able to learn to love, to try to understand" (Lowe, 107). Kelly's voice unifies, explains, edits, and directs reader attention. Because he cannot be present throughout all of the story's action, his narrative is supplemented by eyewitness accounts of others. This tactic enriches the novel by adding voices and drawing on Gaines's rich use of colloquial language. Thus, Kelly becomes the spokesman for everyone—black and white. His humane, often comic commentary, brings a fresh perspective to a potentially melodramatic situation.

Kelly, a plantation tractor driver, becomes an initially unwilling monitor for Marcus when Bonbon assigns him to drive Marcus to Baton Rouge to pick up his belongings. Bonbon also assigns Marcus the room adjoining Kelly's. But the person most responsible for making him Marcus's caretaker is the elderly lady who raised him, Miss Julie Rand. A former cook at the Hebert plantation, Miss Julie has asked Hebert to pay

Marcus's bond, and now she asks Kelly to watch over him. Affirming that Marcus is a "good boy," despite his rude behavior, Miss Julie draws an unwilling but honest commitment from Jim.

Unlike Jackson Bradley of *Catherine Carmier*, Kelly changes during the text as he grows to understand Marcus's position. And it is *not* an easy position to understand since Marcus seems completely self-centered, stubborn, and obstinate to the point of stupidity. Rude and arrogant, he shows contempt and suspicion when Jim feeds him and gives advice. He insults Jim and others, completely ignoring plantation conventions as if he is exempt from all rules. Marcus threatens the order of the plantation community, which remains both incredulous and censorious of his actions. But because Jim is a man of his word, and because he is ultimately influenced by Marcus, he perseveres and attempts to put the whole story together in a retrospective. Wherever he is and whatever he is doing when he tells his story, Jim respects the potential for change that Marcus inspires.

Gaines further enriches the point of view by stressing silence. Again, what people don't say, or what they think as opposed to what they say, plays a significant role. Often, Jim will listen to one speaker and interpret an alternate meaning, having learned to read nuance and indirection. And when Jim hears nothing, he must tell us its particular meaning, for the absence of sound also shifts with its context. Thus Gaines's novel is remarkably economical, spare in its use of words, but rich in the implication of language.

PLOT DEVELOPMENT AND STRUCTURE

As in his first novel, Gaines structures *Of Love and Dust* in three parts, the first establishing character, setting, conflict, and major images. Sitting on the front porch (gallery) of his house, Kelly sees dust coming toward him, and with it the injection of Marcus into his life. Part One takes place during the first week of Marcus's residence on the plantation. It details his rebellious—often contemptuous—attitude and the responses of other plantation residents as they anticipate the trouble he will cause them. Ending with a comically recalled fistfight, Part One also concludes with a small but significant shift of Jim's attitude. Instead of believing in Marcus's ultimate conformity, he now believes that Marcus's spirit will not be broken.

Part Two begins by noting the day and time that Marcus first looks at

Bonbon's wife, Louise, before Jim backs up his narrative to fill in some information. This strategy, which approximates spoken language by circling back to let readers know background, signifies that Jim is "telling" his story to someone. Another indicator that will recur is his question, "would that have done any good?" (135). We know that Jim is haunted by Marcus, that he feels as if he should have done more to help him. And yet his recurring question also suggests his sense of futility, that nothing would have changed events. In this section we begin to see Marcus's character change, along with Jim's, whose character becomes fuller, more introspective, and less self-satisfied. And Gaines also raises the levels of complexity in the two love affairs, illustrating Bonbon's devotion to Pauline and the shift from lust to affection between Marcus and Louise. Frightened by what he sees, Jim continues to encourage conformity to the system of interracial relationships, the complexity and hypocrisy of which few challenge.

In Part Three, the focus broadens, like a pullback camera shot, and readers come to recognize the full ramifications of Marcus's rebellion and the nature of the society he threatens. Thus far, throughout the story, Marcus has inspired anger and fear; now readers see that he challenges an entire social system. Marcus and Louise, emboldened by their love, plan to escape. Meanwhile, Marshall Hebert offers to assist them if Marcus will kill Bonbon, who, having murdered two men for Hebert in the past, has been stealing from him since. Marcus must seem to agree with Hebert, though he doesn't plan to murder Bonbon. By now, Jim begins to see not only the role of conformity in perpetuating the plantation system but also the heroic possibility of Marcus and Louise's actions. More significantly, he doesn't blame Marcus any longer. Instead, he comes to see the active—if subtle—role Hebert plays in pitting black against white, Marcus against Bonbon. He correctly sees Hebert's role in orchestrating both the court verdict of justifiable homicide at Marcus's trial as well as Bonbon's execution of Marcus. In other words, he recognizes Hebert's control not only of the legal system but also the extra-legal system that works to maintain the *status quo*. Jim's final action of the novel suggests his refusal to collude in continuing this unjust system.

The novel's title signifies its major tensions, with dust taking on organizing, suggestive possibilities. Gaines has said that to his mind dust suggests the reverse of love: "Dust is death" (Lowe, 35). Marcus arrives and dies in a cloud of dust. All of the dust in the quarters implies the lack of value placed on its residents, who seem as common and as constant as dust. Plantation owner Marshall Hebert generally arrives and departs in a cloud of dust, signaling the deaths for which he is responsible. Moreover, dust literally and figuratively impairs vision. As long as enough dusts stirs, no one can see Hebert's real role. And since Gaines believes that his characters are determined by society and their environment, dust clouds the thinking of the residents, making Marcus, the outsider whose vision has not yet been blurred, able to see more clearly than people who exist on the plantation (Lowe, 34).

CHARACTER DEVELOPMENT

Jim Kelly's character is important because as the story's narrator, he needs to establish his honesty. At thirty-three, he's old enough to have experienced much of what life has to offer a black man in the restrictive South; yet Jim has learned to move within the system. He describes himself as a man with an eighth-grade education and a sitting-down job. Having established a degree of trust with Sidney Bonbon, Jim nevertheless understands the limits of Bonbon's tolerance. He knows all too well how Bonbon will interpret certain behavior, and he can anticipate with accuracy what Bonbon will do. In fact, Jim's position in the community is central without being an integral part. He has only been on the plantation for three years, giving him something of an outside perspective. But the Hebert plantation is run no differently than other southern plantations in 1947, and thus is a microcosm of the South. Jim sees quite a lot, much of which he disapproves. But he has the good sense born of caution that makes him withhold his judgment—at least around other characters.

He gives readers (and listeners) a good deal of information in drawing the characters involved in his narrative, his insight powerful, his implication clear, if only one listens closely. For instance, he doesn't say that John and Freddie, who work with him in the field, are homosexual, but their actions—giggling, slapping one another, whispering—are quite revealing. Moreover, Jim makes a distinction between "looking at" and "watching." The former suggests overt eye contact, noticeable but without intended action; the latter implies a continuous action with some intent. Thus, readers will be well-advised to look closely at Jim's language because the meanings can be subtle and significant. These language subtleties suggest an intelligence to be admired.

Still, Jim doesn't have a very high opinion of himself. This is due partly to his having accepted his place on the Hebert plantation and the denial of human value his place implies. Everywhere he turns, Jim is reminded that he is less than a white man. He calls attention to the entrances and exits restricted according to color and status, as well as a strict code of behavior. Though he resents going to the "nigger room" in the plantation store, he does not actively protest it. Instead, he will rationalize his acceptance of this racist practice by saying he's too thirsty or tired to do otherwise. Jim's relatively low opinion of himself may also relate to having been abandoned by his wife, Billie Jean, when he couldn't afford the material comforts she demanded. Jim's tender, sexual reveries suggest a level of passionate engagement absent from his present life. But his passive response of her actions also suggests his sense of fatality.

Jim's hopeless acceptance of the system causes Marcus to accuse him of being a "whitemouth," in other words, voicing the opinions of the people in charge. While Jim hotly denies this, Marcus's words sting with truth Jim hasn't yet confronted. To his credit, he takes into consideration Marcus's accusation, and his level of comfort shifts. When he accompanies Bonbon and Pauline to Baton Rouge, he refuses to secure a room for them, admitting that he participates in events: "The Old Man [God] didn't have a thing in the world to do with it. It was me—it was my face" (148). But while rejecting the situation as part of a Divine Plan, he sees himself as a cosmic target: "Anybody who sees this face feels like he ought to use it" (148). Jim's sense of fatality suggests his sense of helplessness, that he has no power to alter events.

But while he has a fatalistic view, Jim nevertheless progresses to accepting some responsibility even while he continues to caution Marcus to follow the direction of others, accept his status, and serve his time. When Marcus challenges Jim with the question, "Where would people be if they didn't take a chance?" (248–49) followed by the story of his education, Jim finally connects with Marcus: "I felt empty because I doubted if I believed in anything, either" (253). Now able to see how much they share, Jim begins to admire Marcus's differences, particularly his "great courage" (270). Marcus's challenge to authority, which has inspired fear and anger, now makes Jim "more proud of Marcus" (271). Thus, when Hebert encourages Jim to leave the plantation and offers a letter of recommendation as payment for silence, Jim refuses. He no longer wants a white warrant of approval, particularly not one from a morally corrupt source. Jim strikes out in his own direction.

He owes his liberation from the shackles of a slave mentality to Marcus, whose example seems problematic at best. Gaines sought to create in Marcus a character who would send shock waves through the system. We see Marcus's rebellious nature overtly through his dress and behavior. Jim's patience is tried over and over by Marcus's unwillingness to conform to plantation life, beginning with his clothes. Against Jim's advice, Marcus refuses to change his city clothes for sturdy khaki work-clothes worn by plantation field hands. By refusing the uniform, Marcus announces his conviction that he is *unlike* other workers. And he is. Marcus's constant refusal to dress like everyone makes his individuality conspicuous, and his actions are consistent with his dress.

His choice takes considerable courage because Marcus is subjected to what can only be described as slave breaking (Babb, 70). Frederick Douglass was perhaps the first to accurately describe the practice which attempts to break the human spirit through demanding physical labor in his *Narrative of the Life of Frederick Douglass.* Marcus's experience is similar to Douglass's in that he is told to perform a task for which he has neither experience nor instruction. And then he is put under very close scrutiny. Anticipating the level of physical discomfort that will come with the assigned labor, Jim makes sure that Marcus has the easiest row of corn to pick, not that there is such a thing as a truly "easy" row on a plantation. All the work is hard, and the physical conditions only make it worse. The weather can be particularly oppressive. In fact, the intense heat of a late south Louisiana summer becomes an active character in this novel. Throughout the novel, Gaines calls careful attention to the reality of physical conditions, and shows how it is used to control behavior.

Marcus manages to maintain a diminished pace during the morning harvest. Just as his energy is exhausted in the afternoon, when the temperature is most intense, Bonbon arrives to remind Marcus of the realities of their relationship. Placing his horse behind Marcus, close enough so that Marcus can feel the horse's breath on his neck, Bonbon stays behind him, not giving him a chance to recover from exhaustive, repetitive labor. Bonbon's tactics are designed for maximum intimidation, as his position atop his horse suggests. And just in case Marcus has any doubts about his authority, Bonbon shoots a hawk to illustrate his power. Marcus struggles through his first week and looks forward to a day of recovery. But he is assigned Saturday afternoon labor which Hebert indicates might continue on Sundays, too—at least until Marcus decides to do Hebert's bidding. Hebert's attempts to turn Marcus into some form of work animal bring tears, suggestive of Marcus's struggling feelings. They do not, however, alter his character.

Marcus's character is perplexing to everyone. From the very first, he offends. Jim is especially put off by his refusal to accept responsibility for the murder he committed. Marcus has killed another black man over a woman, and firmly maintains that he acted in self-defense. Gaines focuses our attention on two key issues here: Marcus's shallow, purely sexual valuation of women, which is in keeping with all of his other self-serving actions; and his accurate interpretation of a social system in which the lives of black men have no value. When Marcus affirms that his victim "was nothing," he is simply stating the obvious and accepted attitude. And he consistently notes the hypocrisy of the legal system that chooses to punish him for eliminating someone who doesn't hold status as a man. But while the social system denies his manhood, Marcus finds a means of affirming himself.

Intent on living as a man, he finds the most obvious way of doing so through his sexuality. Thus, he sets out to seduce Pauline Guerin because she is the most desirable woman on the plantation. Later, he will strike Pauline, not because she refuses him but because she responds to Marcus like "she had seen the devil himself" (118). In other words, Pauline does not respond to him as a man but a monster—something less than human. Only then does Marcus begin thinking of seducing Louise as a means of revenge on Bonbon. Though aware that his choice probably means death, he chooses to live as a man on his own terms. What he doesn't anticipate, however, is learning to feel for a human being other than himself. To his own surprise, Marcus actually falls in love, valuing Louise's devotion and seeing her situation similar to his: "She much slave here as I was" (261). He tries to free Louise at the cost of his own life.

Marcus's heroism is partly due to sheer stubbornness, a quality that can be both irritating and heroic. Gaines emphasizes Marcus's individual stature in many ways, but they all come together in a key scene when Marcus goes to see Marshall Hebert. Though he uses the back door, Marcus omits the "Mister" when asking to see Hebert. Refused entry by Hebert's valet, Bishop, Marcus pushes "his foot . . . in the house slavery built" (215), and conducts his conversation with Hebert as an equal. The outrage that Bishop expresses suggests how deeply he has internalized Hebert's values as well as his blindness to the damage of continuing this system. Somehow, maintaining the house "slavery built" has become as important to Bishop as to Hebert—perhaps more important since Bishop's anger is fiercer than Hebert's.

But Hebert needs Marcus and knows how to use him. As has been mentioned, Hebert is most often seen in a cloud of dust, part of a deliberately vague strategy of characterization. Everyone except Marcus and—much later—Jim is unable to see him and his actions clearly. What we come to understand about this character is through interpreting actions witnessed at a distance and often obscured by obstacles. Gaines's use of distance and indirection increases the sense of ambiguity about Hebert, but this character's association with dust suggests his true nature. We know Hebert to be manipulative, not because of established fact but rather through rumor. Noting that he is an alcoholic and his brother, Bradford, a gambler, we grasp a sense of the family's moral decay, a deterioration that seems to accelerate with time. Late in the novel, we will be told that Hebert has probably arranged for Bonbon to murder a gambler who has insisted on collecting Bradford's debts. Though Bonbon is responsible for only one murder, we are given the impression that he also orchestrated the fight which killed the gambler threatening Hebert. Through the years, Bonbon has used Hebert's debt as a license to steal, with Hebert allowing the theft as the price of Bonbon's silence. Bonbon's presence eats on Hebert, but all his efforts to get Bonbon to leave have been futile. In Marcus, however, Hebert sees another opportunity to rid himself of Bonbon. Hebert uses Bonbon to punish Marcus, expecting and later encouraging Marcus to direct his hatred at Bonbon. During their interview, Hebert denies any responsibility for Bonbon's actions. Like Iago in *Othello*, Hebert claims to befriend Marcus. He acts as if he is innocent of the way Marcus has been treated and seems unabashed by Marcus's plans. In fact, he assures Marcus that he will help him escape. Hebert's denial of responsibility suggests his moral bankruptcy.

Gaines's characterization of Bonbon, Pauline, and Louise is deceptively simple. All might easily become stereotypes, but thanks to Gaines's ability to evoke complexity with remarkable economy, all reveal themselves to be deeply human. Bonbon, particularly, might be read as a simple, brutal man. To Hebert he is a liability, to Marcus an unyielding taskmaster, to Jim a problematic boss. A Cajun with a third-grade education, Bonbon has followed the expected code of behavior. But he walks a fine line between seeming to observe the strict race codes while emotionally violating them. He takes a black woman for his sexual pleasure, but then he moves from sexual exploitation to genuine devotion. And while his culture endorses—in fact encourages—the former, it strictly forbids the latter. Thus, Bonbon can live only on the periphery of his community. Gaines underscores this by pointing out his limited contact with his nearby family as opposed to his closeness to Pauline. Bonbon is rarely at home and most often on the road or in the fields, in transit with no recognized space for himself. Louise occupies his house, and Pauline claims her own home.

That Bonbon is emotionally closer to the very people he has been encouraged to devalue than to his own family is also made plain through his relationship with Jim Kelly, whom Bonbon calls "Geam." In mispronouncing his name, Bonbon seems to denigrate the person and thus undercut their relationship. Ironically, Jim is the only man on the plantation with whom Bonbon can converse and he knows it, revealing his trust when he asks Jim to accompany them to Baton Rouge. Jim's purpose is as a shield, to pose as Pauline's husband. But Bonbon also needs Jim as a guide, to recommend a comfortable place where the three of them can be together. Jim takes them to a bar where people of mixed blood congregate and where Bonbon and Pauline will not be out of place. In fact, Kelly comments that Bonbon is darker than several of the mulatto bar patrons. Gaines depicts the many and complicated paradoxes of established race codes, indicating the mutual dependence of both black and white. While he seems to pay attention to differences, Bonbon recognizes that he shares more with the black residents of the plantation than with the white: "We little people, Geam. They make us do what they want us to do, and they don't tell us nothing"(258).

Even more than her husband, Louise undergoes a transformation of ideology. An abused child, fifteen-year-old Louise is given to Bonbon as a wife. In the subsequent ten years, she has tried to escape her loveless marriage only to be returned to Bonbon. Small, ignorant, and wholly dependent, Louise is depicted as a child; her choice of skirt and blouse as opposed to the dresses adult women wear emphasize her lack of development. Dependent upon Margaret to care for both her and her daughter, Tite, Louise seems to embody the febrile white woman of stereotype until she decides upon her course of action. Having absorbed the mythology of black male sexuality and the contradictory conviction of black male monstrousness, Louise is both terrified and determined. As long as she can look at black men from her porch, she is safe. But when she begins watching Marcus (and he returns her look), she begins to act. Louise progresses in stages, literally touching Marcus to assure her of his humanness, and, later, requiring some sort of bruise as a mark of his presence. But Marcus becomes her true lover, and his sweet talk meets a need that has never been acknowledged, much less met, by other men. Thus, Louise falls in love with a man who treats her with tenderness. Still, she wonders about her own feelings, asking Margaret if it's possible for a white woman to love a black man. As her devotion increases, Louise begins taking chances, risking their lives as they become more public. That their relationship is more than sexual heat is shown in their nakedness before Margaret. There is a genuine innocence in their natural comfort with one another, complementing their naive belief that they can escape the confines of their social system.

Pauline Guerin is given even less voice than other principal characters, part of Gaines's strategy of characterization. Single, black, and female, the physically enticing Pauline is valued by the men on the Hebert plantation primarily for her sexual charms. Because she "belongs" to Bonbon, however, Pauline is marginalized. She must live in the black community, but she's unable to freely interact with its residents as they are with her. Pauline's reputation for courtesy is more than illustrative of her kindness; it's also a form of distance. And her limited speech underscores her social position. But her tasteful dress, graceful walk, and erect posture suggest a substantial woman, and her rambunctious twin sons signify her vitality, particularly in contrast to their frail half-sister, Tite, Bonbon's daughter by Louise. Late in the novel, readers become aware of Pauline's comprehensive understanding of the situation with a simple gesture, when Jim tells her that Marcus and Louise plan to elope: "Pauline covered her mouth with her hand" (257). Her lack of voice indicates her social position at Hebert, where she has little say in what happens to her. Once again, Gaines's use of dress, gesture, and body language says as much or more about characters as their language.

THEMATIC CONCERNS

Gaines's exploration of paradoxical racial distinctions exposes its many and complex ramifications. What makes his dramatization of interracial love affairs different from most fictional treatments is that other novels generally focus on the offspring of interracial love, not the affair itself, the latter being a source of considerable social discomfort (and interest). In fact, an entire fictional sub-genre about the "tragic mulatto" exists (see *Clotel, Autobiography of an Ex-Colored Man, Passing*). Novels that did focus on the love affair often explored its more sensational elements (see *Light in August*). These novels rarely dealt with the effects of interracial relationships on the community other than the violent mob action. And most—if not all—of these novels failed to indicate the cost of these artificially thwarted relationships.

That white men have sometimes loved black women and their children by them is an inescapable fact of American social history. But the cost of these affairs to the individual and the community is a subject social histories cannot explore. *Of Love and Dust* details the reluctance with which Bonbon and Pauline fall in love. Neither wants to because of its emotional price. Pauline must sacrifice not only possible liaisons with black men; she must observe a high degree of discretion with her community, indeed with her closest neighbors, Aunt Caline and Pa Bully. Living next door to Pauline, with no physical barrier on their shared front porch and only a thin, uninsulated wall between rooms, Aunt Caline and Pa Bully must negotiate a selective deafness and self-willed blindness to Bonbon's arrivals and departures. Other characters must also remain aware of Bonbon's plans precisely so they can disappear at the appropriate moment. In fact, there is a good deal of comedy in the continual interest in Bonbon's plans as well as elaborate avoidance of open acknowledgment. Everyone on the plantation knows about them. Certainly, Bonbon's loving Pauline more than Louise is widely acknowledged. Yet everyone also makes some effort not to directly speak of this love on the plantation. Off the plantation, discussion is more open. That's why Miss Julie asks Jim if he thinks "there will ever be a time" when Pauline and Bonbon can live together (14) and why Jim can now tell the entire story.

The impetus for silence over interracial relationships begins in the white community, which has created the restrictions and invented the sanctions. As a devalued female, Pauline may suffer no more than being marginalized by the black community. And this is difficult because everyone recognizes that Pauline has no choice in the matter. She must remain Bonbon's mistress as long as he wants her. For Bonbon, the price of his relationship beyond the purely sexual is extreme. Jim tells us that Bonbon's own brothers might murder him to salvage their family reputation. But the community has considerable practice in ignoring this kind of relationship, so it remains undisturbed.

Marcus's affair with Louise, however, is another matter because it threatens the entire community. While white men allowed themselves the privilege of crossing a color line, they created mortal sanctions against black men who did the same. Whenever Marcus is linked to Louise, the response is that he will be lynched. Lynching involves not simply hanging but burning a man alive, usually after considerable torture and dismemberment. Sexual mutilation also played a major role in this collective act of murder. The corpse would then be hung from a tree as a warning sign to the black community. Blues singer Billie Holliday's

"Strange Fruit" recalls this action in tragic detail. There need not be any actual contact between black man and white woman. Nor would there be much effort to conclusively identify a particular suspect. Often, a mere allegation would be sufficient provocation for black men to be hunted and lynched. Mob rule is always indiscriminate, its waves of violence reverberating through the community. That's why Jim and Margaret work so hard to deter Marcus and why everyone dreads the outcome of their act. Sexual relations are the ultimate violation of white rule, at once disproving the myth of black male monstrousness and endangering white lines of descent. Bonbon may not own property, but any child born to Louise while they are legally married would carry his name. However, disproving the myth of black male inhumanity is the more important issue, because refusing to recognize black men as men is the fundamental premise of slavery. Thus, when Marcus enters Louise's bedroom at her invitation, he creates a fissure that will weaken this ideological foundation.

Gaines emphasizes this by showing Louise's physical reticence. First she watches Marcus, then she timidly touches him. Even after her feelings have deepened, Louise has doubts since she has been taught to believe that such feelings are impossible. Though she recognizes Bonbon's love for Pauline and sees daily evidence of Margaret's love for Tite, Louise cannot extend the similarity to her love for Marcus. But instead of remaining imprisoned by that idea, she determines to free herself from the illusions of the past.

Above everything else, *Of Love and Dust* focuses our attention on what Charles Rowell has termed the "struggles of a static world fiercely resistant to change," that is, on the tension between ideological bondage and freedom (735). If we look closely at the characters Bishop, Margaret, and Jim, we see their differences. Bishop's very name tells us that he is a guardian. He watches over Hebert's house as both sentinel and housekeeper, working to maintain its order and all this implies. His personal attachment to the house is so deep that when Hebert orders Bishop to leave the kitchen, Bishop refuses, reminding Hebert that he has been promised his place as long as he remains a "good boy" (236). More than a residence, though, the big house has become a symbol of the Old South. Gaines's use of the big house recalls the way William Faulkner uses the house Thomas Sutpen designs in *Absalom, Absalom!*. As the emblem of class and authority, its size and position announce the status of its owner. Thus, Bishop's position as guardian means that he believes in the rightness of the system that constructed and maintains the house. The house

has, then, become his ideology, Bishop's means of interpreting and re-
acting to events. Jim tells us that Bishop's faith rests more in the big
house than in church (222), and his observation is borne out when Bishop
prays to the old people for forgiveness after Marcus desecrates the sacred
space by not observing the proprieties. In fact, Bishop is outraged when
Marcus violates "the house slavery built," (215) suggesting faith in a
system that will not recognize him as a man (Hebert still calls him
"boy"). His self-willed bondage binds Bishop more securely to slavery
than any legal system. Though he is a daily witness to the Hebert family
deterioration and has direct knowledge of Marshall Hebert's arrange-
ments, Bishop remains blind to the truth. To sustain the illusion of order,
perpetuate tradition, and support his belief in white superiority, Bishop
must believe Hebert deserving of his position. And to support his faith,
he must absolve him of all responsibility. To the very end, Bishop blames
Marcus for all the trouble on the plantation. Thus, in the end, Jim appropriately sees Bishop as a ghost, a haunting spirit of a dead past.

Margaret's attitudes echo Bishop's, though in a slightly different way.
Like Bishop, she witnesses many actions illustrating human frailty and
thus lack of superiority. Because of her daily closeness to the helpless
Louise, Margaret has every reason to know of her superior skills, wisdom, and judgment. And she doesn't mince words about Marshall Hebert's alcoholism. Still, Margaret does choose to forget his role in order
to achieve a level of safety for herself. She indicates this when she tells
Jim, "When you live long as I done lived, you learn to forget things quite
easy" (279). She ultimately denies Marshall Hebert's role, an act that can
allow her to return to the only world she has known. As she turns back
toward the plantation, Jim sees her going "home," the last word of the
novel and a word resonant with meaning.

Jim, however, moves in another direction. Throughout Parts One and
Two, Jim's position resembles Margaret's. He doesn't challenge tradition,
fearing violence. Paradoxically, Jim wants to strike Marcus much of the
time, literally wanting to knock "sense" into the young man, using violence to force him to conform. But Jim changes his mind when Marcus
shows him what he already knows, that Marshall Hebert orchestrates
what happens on the plantation, not Sidney Bonbon. At this point, Jim
considers the futility of preventing disaster: "But where did you go when
it was the rich white man? You couldn't even go to the law, because he
was the law. He was police, he was judge, he was jury" (198). Marcus
guides Jim, challenging his belief in the system and urging him to see a
possibility for difference. His ultimate challenge comes with his question,

"Where would people be if they didn't take a chance?" (249). But he already knows the certain answer to his question, "Right here in this quarter the rest of they life" (249).

In setting up an opposition between the past and change, Gaines challenges readers to consider the value of the past. The most revered portions of southern tradition emanate from the plantation system which is wholly dependent upon slavery. There is, of course, an illusion of security in this system. Highly structured, authoritarian, with distinct notions of place and role, the plantation system appears safe—even beautiful—especially from distant time and experience. To Bishop and Margaret, it is familiar, its patterns deeply etched in repetitive actions and learned responses. Their need to protect what they know reflects a level of comfort each has created within the system. Despite its demeaning attitudes toward workers, exploitative wage scale, harsh working conditions, and crowded and impoverished quarters, the plantation system has paradoxically created a close and rich community. Charles H. Rowell has explored the implications of place in Gaines's work, calling attention to Gaines's use of the quarters as a "center of meaning" in his novels (749). When Bishop and Margaret defend the old system, they associate it not directly with slavery but with the rich culture slavery engendered. They are defending the recurring rhythms of life that take place after work: making music, visiting with neighbors, holding house parties, going to church. Ultimately, they simply try to hold onto their world, with its shared intimacy. Jim respects their position, though he no longer shares it.

Jim's departure from the plantation at the novel's end suggests a new direction in his life, a life less compliant and fatalistic. Marcus has shown Jim that individual acts can matter, that refusing to be like everyone else is admirable, requiring courage. Of course, Jim has little choice about leaving since Hebert tells him he'd be safer elsewhere. Hebert's implied threat underscores his undiminished power, and it also suggests his fear of Jim. What does Jim know that Hebert wants kept secret? Mostly Jim sees through the artificial restrictions of race to the power that refusing to be limited can offer. He understands that refusing to cooperate with a corrupt system has the potential to damage it. Jim's understanding is identical to the conclusion Henry David Thoreau writes of in "On the Lessons of Civil Disobedience" and to the strategies employed by Mahatma Gandhi and Martin Luther King, Jr. in their civil rights struggles.

Marcus does not change Hebert or the plantation's inhabitants, but he does change Jim and thus opens a possibility for change. Some characters will ignore this opportunity; others will take notice. The end result, though, is movement, not stasis. The plantation is altered by Marcus's presence. Gaines's novels dramatize the slow, incremental shifts that occur in enduring communities, a strategy coming much nearer to actuality than rapid shifts of behavior and opinion or no shifts at all. In one sense *Of Love and Dust* is tragic, with Marcus winding up dead and Louise placed in a state institution for the insane. Somewhere, though, Bonbon, Pauline, and presumably their children are making a different life for themselves. The people at Hebert will resume their daily rhythms, but though they will seem to forget, memory lingers. True, Marcus challenged the underpinning of slavery and personally lost. But in the process he showed people at the plantation that taking chances and affirming individuality are a means to freedom.

A MARXIST READING

Marxist criticism, based on the principles of German social critics and philosophers Friedrich Engles and Karl Marx, is a set of political, social, and economic ideas that people use to interpret their world. This theoretical lens did not originate as a means of interpreting literature. Rather, it began in the nineteenth century as a practical interpretation of human history, one including the role of the working classes, and would become the basis of socialism and communism. In *The Communist Manifesto* (1848) Marx and Engles begin with the premise that reality is material; that is, what we see, hear, feel, taste, and touch comprises reality. Since people live in social groups, Marxists believe that cultural and social circumstances determine who we are. In other words, our cultural and social circumstances tell us how to think about ourselves and others, they determine our values, and they instruct us in what to believe. Dividing people into the "haves" (capitalists or the bourgeoisie) and the "have nots" (the working class or proletariat), Engels and Marx showed how the "haves" enslaved the "have nots" through economic policies and control of production. Further, they argue that the "have nots" should rise in rebellion, take the economic control from the "haves," and invest ownership of all property in the hands of the government. Only then will material wealth be equally distributed (Bressler, 116).

In a later work, *Das Kapital* (1867), Marx presented his predictably economic interpretation of history. When people engage in manufacturing goods, for example weaving cloth, making plows, or growing food, they form social relationships. The many, who actually produce material goods, have little control over the few people who employ them. Thus, the few (the "haves") gain not only material but social and political control of their society. The "haves" influence more than economic policy and production, however. Because they control such human institutions as government, education, and religion, they also control the artistic expression of any culture, including its literature.

Marxist ideology played some role in literary interpretation during the 1920s and especially the 1930s, when many American and European intellectuals believed that Marxism held the key to bringing their nations out of a deep economic depression. These critics often attacked authors on the basis of their ideas, not their literary art, and were particularly judgmental of authors whose writing ignored working-class sympathies. But in the wake of the Cold War, this ideology fell into disrepute. In the politically restless days of the early 1970s, however, both European and American critics found in Marxism a way of understanding and interpreting social discontent. Viewing society—even a fictional society—through a Marxist lens means, first of all, understanding the motivating ideology behind human action and its effects on society. Secondly, Marxist critics seek to discover which phenomena actually dominate life. This is why Marxist literary critics focus on an author's world view and the sociological implications of a text as opposed to conventional literary devices. Such an analysis of ideology, Marxist critics believe, will expose the concerns (and thus the agenda) of either the "haves" or the "have nots" (Bressler, 174). Ira Schor offers a series of questions Marxist critics ask in a *College English* article, questions referring to the kind of social critique a novel raises, the origin of a work's conflicting sources, and the values of specific social classes. These principally thematic issues guide readers in seeing a work's relation to society (179).

A Marxist reading of *Of Love and Dust* will focus on the implications of the plantation system depicted by Gaines. Clearly it is a corrupt system, depending upon the underpaid labor of many for the comfort of the dissolute Marshall Hebert. Hebert's secretive movements, his control of other people, manipulation of the legal system for his own benefit, lack of conscience and sense of responsibility, and unchallenged authority are exposed in Gaines's novel, clearly not written by a member of the ruling class.

The novel's conflicting forces seem embodied in Marcus and Bonbon, with each man attempting to express the values of his race and class. Bonbon, however, is revealed as a mere shield for Marshall Hebert. Not only does Bonbon not share Hebert's social class, his values are shown to be similar to those of Jim and Marcus. He is, as Jim will point out, "only a tool" for Marshall Hebert, like Marcus, like Jim, and all the other plantation workers. Looking at this story, one might explore both educational and economic opportunities of Louisiana, exposing the built-in limitations. Or one might examine the socioeconomic conflicts between poor whites and poor blacks. Another reading might direct reader attention to the legal system and its effects in the text.

Marshall Hebert, then, representing the ruling class, would attract particular scrutiny, with emphasis on his value system. One of the principal claims of southern aristocracy is its high valuation of manners and gentility. Above everything (and everyone), Marshall Hebert is supposed to be a gentleman; it's both his status and his value system. Among the genteel skills valued by the old South are riding, drinking, and gambling with skill and good manners. Hebert's refusal to honor his brother Bradford's gambling debts violates the ruling class code of honor. Moreover, it reveals the true nature of Hebert's value system—inherently greedy and self-centered. The length to which Marshall Hebert is willing to go to preserve his status is extreme, as we see in his arranged murders of the gambler, Bonbon, and Marcus. Clearly, he values no life beyond his own. Thus, Hebert's claim to any form of superiority is revealed to be invalid, his rule corrupt and deserving of revolution.

Marcus Payne threatens Hebert and the exploitative system he represents through the simple and heroic affirmation of his own human value. In refusing to become Hebert's tool, first as a field worker and later as a hired killer, Marcus poses a direct threat to the authority Hebert claims. Unimpressed by social conventions, Marcus determines his own value system, but only after he is properly educated in how the system works. Though he begins by believing what adults tell him about the power of the white man, Marcus changes his mind when he is cheated and threatened, his prayers and confidence unrewarded by faith. When his church congregation breaks into laughter after hearing his prayers that Big Red stop taking his money, Marcus changes his strategy and attacks Big Red. But the legal system simply takes his education a step further, duplicating the kind of extortion Big Red practiced. Everywhere he turns, Marcus is victimized by representatives of the ruling class (the white man) through the "white man's nigger" (252), suffering physical abuse in the process. He chooses to resist the system, rather than contribute to it, because he sees that "it don't add up to nothing but a big pile of shit" (253). His value system becomes entirely self-centered and self-directed until he falls in love with Louise. Though not a classic Marxist hero—that is, one who might be an inspiration to oppressed workers and leader of revolutionary actions—Marcus nevertheless exposes the corrupt nature of the plantation system.

Key to this system is denial of human value for virtually everyone but the land owners. Every character in the novel is therefore reduced to a level where Hebert thinks no more of interfering with their lives than he would breaking a glass. Their only value is in his particular use for them as cook, overseer, field worker, or murderer. Hebert's means of control to encourage conformity to his system are pervasive, as we see through his ability to orchestrate not only Marcus's trial date but also the verdict. When the legal system cannot meet his needs, he can manipulate working-class whites as terrorists. Death and exile continue as threats to anyone failing to conform to the system, their presence so imminent they shadow basic human impulses of love and justice. Whatever solidarity exists among the field workers is quickly eclipsed by fear for their own lives.

Discussion of the love interests would doubtless focus more on the implications of caste as a means of control than on the social response each couple inspires. Marcus and Louise's growth in learning to care for each other might be less important to a Marxist critic than the unjustness of a system that first enslaves them and then mercilessly disposes of them when they fail to conform. And Jim Kelly's key role as narrator would have less significance than his role as inheritor of Marcus's rebellious legacy. *Of Love and Dust* readily lends itself to a Marxist interpretation because its narrative focuses in such detail on the prevailing social system in south Louisiana during the 1940s, a time of slow transition, with oppressive nineteenth-century values retaining hold on many residents. In setting up the dichotomies between worker and owner, Gaines gives readers an opportunity to see a system from a differing perspective.

5

The Autobiography of Miss Jane Pittman
(1971)

When discussing the inception of *The Autobiography of Miss Jane Pittman*, Gaines says that he wanted to write a "folk biography" and that he wrote at least one draft with "a group of people telling of this one person's life" over 100 years of history (Lowe, 101). But this version struck Gaines as "untrue," so he proceeded to write from the character's point of view—with a little help from her friends. Inspired by the strong, determined character of his Aunt Augustine Jefferson, to whom the novel is dedicated, *The Autobiography of Miss Jane Pittman* draws on the tradition of the slave narrative and its creative branch, the fictional autobiography.

Slave narratives are essentially stories of enslavement, suffering, endurance, and escape. A formula for organizing the telling of stories by slavery's victims was devised by abolitionists, who used personal testimonies of escaped slaves to influence public opinion. Most accounts remained oral, but several notable exceptions were published in the nineteenth century, especially the narratives of Frederick Douglass (*Narrative of the Life of Frederick Douglass, My Life and Times, The Life and Times of Frederick Douglass*). The artistry of his account continues to give depth and insight to the slave experience. Women's stories were also a part of this literary tradition, specifically *Incidents in the Life of a Slave Girl* by Harriet Jacobs. Quite early at least one writer chose to tell her story in "fictional" form. Harriet Wilson's *Our Nig* (1859) draws on the slave narrative tradition and closely follows the factual details of Wilson's life but asks readers to believe the story is fiction. Prior to Gaines's work, James Weldon Johnson had written his powerful *Autobiography of an Ex-Colored Man* (1910), a novel posing as another genre. These accounts speak for a group through the experience of individuals, testifying to the remarkable ingenuity of the oppressed and often drawing upon deep religious convictions. So one can readily see how deeply rooted the related literary traditions of personal and fictionalized narrative are for African American writers. Gaines has said that he found the proper approach for his novel when he read Gertrude Stein's *The Autobiography of Alice B. Toklas* (Lowe, 303). Trying to create an authentic "voice" while writing *The Autobiography of Miss Jane Pittman* Gaines studied the language of slave narratives, collected in WPA interviews with former slaves in *Lay My Burden Down* (Gaudet, "Miss Jane and Personal Experience," 30). His novel draws together the voices and actions of a displaced population at the end of the Civil War to weave a strong fabric of community and commitment alive with the colors and textures of human endurance.

POINT OF VIEW

The key to understanding this novel's strategy is found in the "Introduction," a literary pose which foregrounds the text. During the summer of 1962, a fictional historian in south Louisiana approaches Miss Jane Pittman asking to tape-record her story. Initially reluctant, Miss Jane agrees to talk only after the historian explains that he believes her story will "help . . . explain things to my students, things that aren't in" the books he uses to teach. The trouble with these books, he continues, is that "Miss Jane is not in them" (vi), suggesting pointedly that she should be. His initial certainty of completing the project in two weeks fades as over the next nine months he continues to accrue material. The historian quickly discovers that constructing a life isn't a simple, straightforward process, as friends of Miss Jane fill memory lapses, correct errors, and add stories, stories the historian finds increasingly out of control. Instead of a neat, linear narrative, what emerges is increasingly messy, frustrating the historian, who ultimately sees the wisdom of Mary Hodges' explanation that "you don't tie up all the loose ends all the time" (vii). Thus, when he reconstructs the story in his role as editor, the historian pays homage to all of the people who contributed because "Miss Jane's story is all of their stories, and their stories are Miss Jane's" (viii).

Although Gaines initially employed multiple points of view for *The Autobiography of Miss Jane Pittman*, envisioning a "series of conversations after Miss Jane has died" (Lowe, 61), he was disappointed with the result. In rewriting from a first-person perspective, he encountered the usual limitation that angle of narration automatically creates: how one person can plausibly know all kinds of information. The solution to his problem lies in the creation of the historian/editor of the novel's "Introduction," a character who explains how the entire community comes to share Miss Jane's story, making it their own.

Using first-person point of view, Gaines has to create language that "sounds" authentic while being intelligible to readers. He therefore has Jane pronounce certain words as she hears them: "sable" for "sabre," "beero" for "bureau," "whas" for "wasp." More often, he depends upon syntax and colloquialisms to flavor the language, giving Miss Jane's voice a distinctive sound that readers do not question. Wanting Miss Jane to be intelligent and informed but aware of the limitations she would naturally have, living when she did, Gaines devised a method of digesting large amounts of historical information. His research while writing this novel included reading histories, black folklore, and interviews with former slaves, information that Miss Jane might be aware of though she would remain illiterate. Describing his character as "very knowing from a folk, noneducated point of view," Gaines knew he needed a "verbal format" and thus decided to use the idea of a tape recorder (Lowe, 139).

What happens over the course of the novel is quite interesting because the book includes vivid details from Jane's experiences—for example, the first scene when she waters both Confederate and Union troops, the massacre in the woods which she and Ned survive, their subsequent wanderings toward Ohio, her attempts to save Joe Pittman's life, and her metaphorical travels when she gets religion. Then there are instances where a tape recorder seems to run as Jane's voice becomes that of the entire community. The "we" of Book IV is a collective point of view. This tape recorder also serves another purpose, allowing access to actions Jane couldn't possibly witness such as Robert Samson's accusation of Mary Agnes and Jimmy's attempted seduction of Eva. As Jane ages, she naturally becomes more observer than actor. Living in a small, isolated community where news, usually focused on the private details of others' lives, is routinely passed around, Jane would naturally become a living repository of these kinds of details. In the end, her narrative perspective becomes a kind of filter and conduit as information passes through her.

Gaines's creation was so successful, his rendering of Jane's voice so convincing, that many readers came to believe that Jane was a living person, not a fictional character (Gaudet, "Miss Jane and Personal Experience," 24).

PLOT DEVELOPMENT AND STRUCTURE

Miss Jane's story is divided into four books entitled "The War Years," "Reconstruction," "The Plantation," and "The Quarters." As the narrative moves forward in a fairly orderly manner, other movements transpire within the text. Moving from national expanses of time and political upheaval into the relatively small Quarters, the book titles seem to narrow as the novel's action broadens, moving away from Jane into the voices and actions of others. This seems logical given that the hero of this novel is 110 years old. Another way of viewing the book's structure is in seeing it centered not only around Jane but also around the four men in her life: Ned, Joe Pittman, Tee Bob, and Jimmy. This double perspective does not relegate Jane to any reduced significance; rather, it helps readers to see her as a character whose unconscious and unplanned leadership emerges, illustrating the truth of Miss Jane's words to Jimmy late in the novel, "People and time bring forth leaders" (228). Seen from this angle, the novel's moral center remains the character of Jane while the male characters illustrate challenges to social positions. The male characters, then, provide one example of leadership while Miss Jane provides another.

The title of the first book, "The War Years," seems initially misleading since the novel quickly moves into the postwar period. But in south Louisiana, the war continues long after the cessation of shooting. Actually, only one chapter of the novel transpires during the Civil War, and it's quite revealing of images and phrases which will recur. At this time, ten- or eleven-year-old Jane is called Ticey, and is commanded by her mistress to draw water for troops, first the retreating Confederate soldiers and then the advancing Union army. When the "Secesh Army" arrives, Jane recalls the ragged dress and exhaustion of the troops. One phrase she overhears particularly strikes her; one of the Confederates says, "Just left to me I'll turn them niggers loose" (4), suggesting a lack of enthusiasm on the part of the enlisted man. But when the Confederates leave, Jane's mistress cries, "Sweet, precious blood of the South" (5). For Jane's white mistress, whose husband hides in a nearby swamp with their family silver and slaves, only the blood of white nobles has value. Soon after the Union army departs, this same character will demand Jane's blood for her insistence upon her new name. And this character's attitude will echo through successive personages and time periods as African Americans begin to claim first their selfhood and then their place in this country. More blood will be shed during the novel—much of it by slavery's victims—and all of it precious to someone.

The "Introduction" also injects one of the novel's dominant and recurrent images, a man on a horse. An emblem of the old South, this image is fraught with suggestive possibilities that recall the chivalric tradition so much a part of southern mythology. Faulkner's *Absalom, Absalom!* uses this image extensively, trying to reconcile the heroic Thomas Sutpen with the flawed mortal he is. Mounted figures in art and literature often suggest authority, as they do in *The Autobiography of Miss Jane Pittman*. The horse helps to distinguish social position, and in many instances indicates attainment of some sort of leadership position. Often, the type of horse suggests something essential about the mounted figure, stallions having particularly emblematic significance. Generals, for example, are not depicted astride mares or draft horses. For nineteenth-century men—especially southern men—the ability to ride well was evidence of manhood. Gaines gives readers another view of this image, one tempered by experience of those who don't ordinarily ride.

In Book I the significant image of a man on a horse will appear in the mounted Patrollers who massacre Jane's party of newly freed people. In Book II, as the people begin to literally reconstruct their lives, this image will take the shape of Joe Pittman in his chosen role of "Chief" wrangler. Joe's insistence upon his manhood automatically puts him at risk. Only by attempting the most hazardous of tasks can he gain respect, but his life is a price he's willing to pay rather than accept lesser status. His death by a black stallion signifies that the time has not yet come for his survival on those terms.

Book III, "The Plantation," focuses attention on "Two Brothers of the South," Timmy and Tee Bob. Both sons of plantation owner Robert Samson, Timmy must nevertheless accept lesser status because his mother, Verda, is black. So even if everyone on the plantation knows who his father is, despite his physical resemblance to his father, although he is athletically superior to his younger, frailer half-brother, and rides a horse while Tee Bob rides a pony, Timmy must ride *behind* his brother. Conversely, the prank both boys play on Jane in this chapter will feature a runaway horse, with Jane's position as rider invoking laughter, not respect. Though Jane does ride, her position commands no respect because of gender.

The man on a horse will reemerge later in the section when Tee Bob falls in love with Mary Agnes LeFabre. Now a young man, Tee Bob remains partially oblivious to the unspoken rules of southern class and caste. Smitten by the beauty and bearing of Mary Agnes, he courts her while riding his horse. As long as he maintains the illusion of superiority (Tee Bob riding his horse while Mary Agnes walks beside), no one interferes with their relationship. But when Tee Bob goes to Mary Agnes, orders her to ride beside him in his car, signifying a sense of equality, and offers his name through marriage, he threatens the social order.

By Book IV, the image fades as horses are replaced by automobiles— even in the Quarters. The disappearance of this image also signals a shifting social climate since Book IV focuses on the creation (and need) for a leader as the people begin to claim their civil rights. In the end, both Robert Samson and Miss Jane are standing on level ground looking at each other. Jane's choice of language indicates a position of equality when she says, "Me and Robert looked at each other there a long time, then I went by him" (246). In positioning the pronoun "me" before Samson and by using only his first name, Jane's language does not defer to Samson's status. More significant, though, is what happens. When Jane moves past Samson, she indicates a complete lack of fear. In the end, his position no longer threatens her.

CHARACTERIZATION

In creating Jane's character, Gaines drew upon the moral strength of his Aunt Augustine, whose courage in the face of physical challenges continues to command his admiration. When he speaks of Miss Augustine Jefferson, Gaines invariably cites her physical endurance, her gritty determination, and an absolute lack of self-pity—characteristics he gives to Jane. From the very beginning, Jane's character shows a stubborn determination that will not be broken, though her owner tries. Soon after the Union troops leave, the recently renamed Jane refuses to answer to Ticey, her slave name. Asserting that she will now be addressed as "Miss Jane Brown," she adds that if the Mistress doesn't like it, Jane will call back Corporal Brown (9). For her act of insolence, Jane will suffer a terrible beating, but she clings, nevertheless, to her new name. This stubborn determination will lead her away from this plantation immediately after freedom is announced, and will sustain both Jane and Ned during their wanderings "North" in a futile attempt to reach Ohio. Her tenacity is responsible for Jane's being able to accept countless hardships without lapsing into self-pity. Another of Jane's most significant characteristics is her sassiness. Meekness simply isn't a factor in her character. Thus, Jane will talk back to her owner, insist on going to Ohio without knowing how to get there, take on women's work before she is twelve years old, and speak out on her behalf and others to those who would prefer silence or humility.

Of course, in order to survive, Jane must learn the all-important lesson of listening. She has refused to hear the wisdom of others who point out her lack of experience, her youth and ignorance, even the dangers of the journey she has undertaken. After days of wandering with Ned, though, Jane recognizes her error when an old man tries to show her where Ohio is on a map: "All of a sudden it came to me how wrong I had been for not listening to people" (48). Fortunately for readers, Jane doesn't immediately mend her ways, for to do so would not simply be out of character, it would deprive readers of one of the novel's finest scenes as the old man procedes to show Jane the way to Ohio, taking into consideration her refusal ever to turn south or move east through Mississippi. Patiently accepting her objections, the old man addresses Jane's question of how long their journey will take, pointing out that Ned won't survive and Jane will be thirty years older before she gets to Cincinnati. Even then Jane refuses to take his answer seriously. Another week of wandering with Ned without any real progress will finally drive the lesson home. Then she decides to listen to what other people have to say.

Learning to listen helps Jane become more flexible, another significant survival trait. After this, she will make decisions based on practical options rather than blind desires, and she will bend in the face of brutal authority rather than break. Knowing that she lacks both the physical strength and political status to take on the Ku Klux Klan and a self-serving legal establishment after various threats and Ned's murder, Jane seems to yield. But it's important to note that she neither succumbs to the views of a prejudical "justice" system nor becomes a cynic.

Jane illustrates her strength of character throughout the novel, particularly when she glosses over her inability to bear children, her legacy of slavery. Jane's barrenness almost prevents her acceptance of Joe Pittman's proposal, but it also spurs her into becoming a mother figure in a much broader sense than having physically given birth. In many respects she becomes a mother to the community, sharing her material goods, experiences, perceptions, energy, and love. We see this literally when she assumes the mothering role of Ned. Later, she will be a stepmother to Joe Pittman's two daughters.

But this part of Jane's life receives scant attention, and the focus is placed instead on Jane's larger role as community mother. Without calling attention to herself, Jane provides a source of humor, wisdom, and acceptance, as changes gradually occur over decades. Though her title as church mother is rescinded because of her refusal to temper her language, Jane is the one Jimmy turns to for support. He knows that she is the moral heart of her community. Despite her age and increasing infirmity, Jane can see the value and the urgency of Jimmy's request that she be a part of their protest. Without pushing herself forward, she announces that she will be present at the demonstration—even when authorities have learned of the planned protest and arrested the young woman chosen to drink from the "whites only" water fountain. Her internal monologue addressed to Jimmy underscores her understanding of community resistance to protest. Nevertheless, Jane sees the importance of Jimmy's plan and insists upon keeping her promise—regardless of danger. Her quiet example of leadership becomes evident as people join her on the morning of the protest, though she gives Jimmy the credit. Even Robert Samson's announcement of Jimmy's murder fails to deter her. In fact, this announcement inspires her final triumph.

Jane's is not a flashy conflict resulting in Samson's acknowledgment of defeat or indeed any conscious recognition that she represents a just position. That's far too unrealistic for Gaines. Instead, Jane's victory is tempered by Gaines's recognition of the limits of social progress as white society has gradually come to recognize the civil and social rights of African Americans. But when Jane looks Samson in the eye, suggesting a sense of social equality, and then moves past him, she illustrates that his threats and commands no longer carry valid authority. In the end, Robert Samson loses his strength because Jane refuses to fear him. Her courage goes beyond words, and her leadership proceeds without bluster.

Gaines draws Jane's character with memorable fullness and depth, imbuing her with the flaws and virtues of a whole people. As for the male characters of this novel, they are more thinly drawn. Nevertheless, they do carry a good deal of thematic weight. Ned, for example, appears only in small scenes, but his character is rich with significance. After his mother and baby sister are murdered by the patrollers, Ned carries the flint and iron that Big Laura has brought with her. This fire-making capacity is both literal and figurative, for later Ned will try to enlighten people so that they can improve their lives. His work with a committee informing poor blacks of ways to escape the *de facto* slavery of Louisiana attracts Klan notice and threats. Instead of retreating, Ned moves to Kansas, gains more education, and resolves to return to carry forward his plan to educate. His return will pose an even greater threat to an entrenched social system dependent upon ignorance.

The fire Ned carries signifies light, and his choice of name signifies his role of leader. Readers are told that Ned changes his name from Ned Brown to Ned Douglass to Ned Stephen Douglass, indicating a choice of political perspective. The threat Ned carries is in his language, for the education he brings with him isn't limited to reading and writing. His convictions regarding the place of Americans of African descent run counter to the political and social attempts to keep these same Americans marginal and landless. Ned's subsequent sermon by the river, reminiscent of the Sermon on the Mount, develops the idea of shared responsibility. He emphasizes the need for mutual respect, because "America is for all of us . . . and all of America is for all of us" (109). Though Ned doesn't denigrate Booker T. Washington's strategy of social appeasement through vocational education and social separation, he clearly supports W.E.B. Du Bois's more radical position of equal rights and opportunities (see Washington's Atlanta Exposition Address and *The Souls of Black Folks*). Concluding his remarks, Ned acknowledges that he will be killed for his convictions, but he's not afraid to die.

Ned's strength of character, his need to claim his own life in a nation that denies him this right, and his insistence upon expressing his integrity are again reflected in the character of Joe Pittman. While Joe has a limited appearance in the story, his name and spirit are a major part of the novel. He exemplifies what black men must face in affirming their independence and manhood. The issue of manhood frequently occurs in works by male authors, and often predominates in those of African American writers, probably because respect for black manhood has long been denied. Accorded a subservient status, black men have historically had fewer employment opportunities, been paid less, accorded less authority, and have been given less respect in the work place than other male workers. Joe Pittman refuses to accept this status, and his character illustrates both the risk and the price black men take in affirming their independence and manhood. Eager to escape the despotic Colonel Dye, Joe literally purchases his freedom with money advanced by Mr. Clyde. This act, which Keith Byerman says is Joe's means of holding "clear title to himself," frees him to develop himself as he sees fit, not as others would have him. ("Historical Fiction," 110). His position as a wrangler on Clyde's ranch earns him status based on ability, not race. Joe is proud of his title, "Chief," recognizing it as a sign of respect since he must face injury—even death—in riding the most dangerous horses. During their ten years on the Texas-Louisiana border, Joe remains impervious to Jane's pleas that he quit to become a farmer. He is no good at farming, and besides, as Chief he doesn't take orders from anyone, he insists.

The black stallion Clyde and his crew capture in Texas signifies an untamed natural spirit virtually all the men admire. Jane takes one look at the horse, has a premonition of Joe's death, and goes to visit Madame Gautier, a hoodoo, who explains the horse to Jane in these words: "Man must always search somewhere to prove himself. He don't know everything is already inside him" (95). Jane's subsequent attempts to save Joe's life prove futile because her stubborn strength of character is matched by his own, and he believes he must ride this stallion. Though the stallion kills Joe and is ultimately broken by another wrangler, the memory of the horse's free spirit—a spirit reflective of Joe Pittman—remains. Throughout her life, Jane carries Joe's name, showing her continuing love and respect.

Tee Bob Samson might seem an unlikely hero, but his presence in the novel is an essential part of Gaines's fictional fabric. Appearing in Book III, Tee Bob first illustrates the theme of brotherhood in his devotion to his half-brother, Timmy. Gaines provides a good deal of comedy in this section, exploiting the gap between what people actually know (that Timmy is Robert Samson's son by the black woman, Verda) and what they can publicly acknowledge (that Timmy is Verda's son—without mention of his father). Robert Samson clearly believes in the old system of which he seems to be master, and his wife, Miss Amma Dean, appears to be accepting of his position. That Timmy is a mirror image of Robert while Tee Bob ("Tee" is a shortening of "petite," meaning "little") more closely resembles his mother, however, signals a movement toward change.

Small, delicate, and sensitive, Tee Bob as a child is drawn to Jane, carrying her cotton sack or urging her to warm herself. He orchestrates Jane's move from field worker to cook, seeing in her a friend he needs. Tee Bob also loves his brother, Timmy, and is both bereft and confused when Timmy is sent away from the plantation after he fights Tom Joe, the overseer. Though the entire family—with the exception of his father—attempts to explain the social dynamic at work, Tee Bob doesn't understand. But Robert, believing that these unspoken rules and expectations of behavior based on race are "a part of life, like the sun and the rain . . . and Tee Bob would learn them for himself when he got older" (147), never attempts to articulate why a brute like Tom Joe is privileged over his own son.

Gaines expands his characterization of Tee Bob by interjecting two significant chapters. These apparent digressions, placed between his childhood and young manhood, give readers both history and metaphor for the events that will follow. In the chapter entitled "Of Men and Rivers," Jane recalls the dreadful and historic flood of 1927, noting that it was caused by human attempts to control water. This observation leads Jane to recall how the old people and Indians had worshipped the water, recognizing its power and nobility. Refusing to respect the river's nature, white men insist upon harnessing its energies for their purposes through a levee system which ultimately intensifies the flood damage. In their need to control, white men refuse to listen to or respect the nature of other forces, a trait that has additional, similarly disastrous consequences. Their blindness leads to destruction on a massive scale during the floods of 1912, 1926, and 1927. On a personal level, it leads to the disaster of Tee Bob's falling in love.

Tee Bob's choice of love interest, Mary Agnes Le Fabre, carries a good deal of racial history, for her immediate family descends from a grandmother, purchased at an octoroon ball in New Orleans by a wealthy white man named Le Fabre. This union apparently becomes a loving one, resulting in the continuence of Le Fabre's name as well as his providing for his nonwhite family by leaving them property, including slaves. But Mary Agnes, in trying to compensate for her slave-holding ancestors, chooses to leave her Creole family to teach black children on the Samson Plantation. Her willingness to sacrifice for her convictions costs her the support of her family.

Struck by Mary Agnes's beauty, Tee Bob finds himself pulled to her despite the various obstacles present, including his commute from Baton Rouge, Mary Agnes's job, Jane's active discouragement, and Mary Agnes's emotional distance. As long as Tee Bob doesn't announce his love, he and Mary Agnes are left alone, though their activities are closely observed. But when he confesses his feelings to his best friend, Jimmy Caya, Tee Bob violates the white male social code. Jimmy asks him, "Don't you know *who* you are? Don't you know *what* she is?" [emphasis mine] (173). His pronoun choices reveal centuries of prejudice in which only white people are accorded human status while black people are reduced to things. Moreover, in Jimmy's mind, a mind reflective of the prevailing social conscience of the time, Mary Agnes is "a nigger" who, despite looking white, has "Africa in her veins" (173). He suggests that Tee Bob's sexual use of her is acceptable, but not his recognition of her as a partner in marriage. Tee Bob reacts with uncharacteristic physical violence, hitting his friend, who nevertheless goes on to emphasize the generally unspoken social codes regarding black women and white men. In articulating a racist code, Jimmy Caya damages Tee Bob's innocence but fails to convert him.

Rather, it's Mary Agnes's refusal to elope with Tee Bob that seems to drive him over the edge to despair and suicide. In appearing to confirm Caya's views, Mary Agnes destroys Tee Bob's hope. As she attempts to explain the code, she recognizes his essential innocence. Readers are told that she talks to him "the way you talk to a child" (176). But her language also indicates Tee Bob's unconscious observations of racial strictures. "That's why," she notes, "you never asked me to get in there [the car] before. . . . That's why you never asked me to get on the horse with you . . ." (176). Tee Bob's subsequent sexual assault so unnerves him that he returns to his home, locks himself in the library, and commits suicide. One might speculate that his physical response to Mary Agnes merely confirms what Caya has described as Tee Bob's "right," but apparently his recognition of what his action says about him becomes the ultimate cause of his death. He elects not to live at all rather than live the life that social convention dictates. His letter to his mother confirms Mary Agnes's innocence. However, without the intervention of Jules Reynard, Mary Agnes would simply become another innocent victim, blamed by a biased system for a murder she doesn't cause.

Only Jules Reynard has the moral courage to stand against Robert Samson's simplistic view of "justice," and he threatens Robert with public exposure if he tries to harm Mary Agnes. Extracting a chain of events from Jimmy Caya, Reynard hears Caya justifying his advice to Tee Bob, in these words: "I didn't tell him no more than what my daddy told me. . . . What my daddy's daddy told him. . . . No more than the rules we been living by ever since we been here" (190). Later, Reynard will add the rest of the community as being culpable in Tee Bob's death. Everyone is involved in a virtual conspiracy to get rid of Tee Bob. Thus, Tee Bob's character suggests more than one might think from a casual reading. In his ability to remain innocent of "rules" based on a medieval idea of the lord of the manor having the right to sexually appropriate any lower-class woman of his choosing, Tee Bob unwittingly threatens an entire social system. Just like the flood of 1927, his emotions overflow an elaborate system of unspoken rules, proving too strong for any artificial boundaries. The resulting disaster leaves its mark on the land and the hearts of those involved.

Tee Bob's character clearly signals change in the system, change that concludes in the character of Jimmy, who appears in Book IV. Jane begins her narrative in this section by referring to a need for a leader, perhaps a savior. Her language indicates a certain mystery, referring to this leader as "the One" (199). Coupled with the enigma of Jimmy's father, readers quickly recognize a connection between Jimmy and Christ—at least as it exists in the minds of the community. Jane acknowledges that the people in the Quarters select Jimmy "because we needed somebody" (200). As that "somebody," Jimmy becomes a symbolic character who is a representative of community need, of communal salvation.

Therefore, the chapters featuring Jimmy have more to do with his training than with him as an individual. It's the 1930s when, in a highly symbolic victory for African Americans, black heavyweight boxer Joe Louis knocks out the reigning champion, Max Schmeling. Jimmy is selected on the heels of this victory to signify challenge and hope. Chastised for any perceived wrongdoing, forbidden to fight, corrected for naturally unruly behavior, Jimmy is embraced and nurtured by the adults of the Quarters, who use Christ as their model. Forbidden expression of his sexual development, he becomes a young man bearing the weighty expectations of his community.

While Jimmy grows, the plantation system changes, becoming more mechanized, resulting in the displacement of field hands. More and more people are forced off the land, including Jimmy's mother. Jimmy joins her shortly after Washington passes a desegregation law (this is probably a reference to the Supreme Court ruling in *Brown v. Board of Education* in 1954) in order to continue his education. Away from his community, Jimmy seems to change, becoming more politicized instead of religious. Jane's narrative reveals that while the South experiences a social upheaval during the Civil Rights movements of the 1950s, the white people of south Louisiana remain arrogantly certain that racial change will not affect their territory. Jimmy's reappearance will shake this illusion.

He returns having found his own voice, having recognized the limits of his strength, and having been convinced of the need to fight. His character fuels a communal conversation among church members expressing real dangers and justifiable fears. But his character also impels action. Approaching Jane, Jimmy appeals for her personal help. He draws her into a plan to demonstrate the degree of racial injustice present as well as its casual acceptance. Knowing that any black person will be arrested for drinking from the "whites only" water fountain, Jimmy secretly arranges for a young girl to perform this gesture of defiance. Comparing her to Miss Rosa Parks, Jimmy wants to use the anticipated overreaction for its public exposure, and he needs Jane to bear and to bring witnesses.

That Jimmy is more spirit than character is suggested by both his absence from the action and his presence in the minds of the people who inhabit the Quarters. Alive, Jimmy provides hope in speculation about his role in the future; dead, he illustrates where the strength lay all along. As Jane concludes, "Just a little piece of him is dead. . . . The rest of him is waiting for us in Bayonne" (245). His martyrdom having solidified the shaky resolve of some, Jimmy's character now inhabits everyone. They begin to claim legal rights as citizens.

THEMATIC CONCERNS

Because Gaines's characters carry so much thematic weight, separating character development from the ideas they dramatize can be both artificial and misleading. But for readers looking for a distinct discussion of the main ideas, it may be helpful to point out that *The Autobiography of Miss Jane Pittman* consolidates many of the issues of Gaines's earlier works, making it almost comprehensive in scope.

As already mentioned, manhood is a significant theme in its personal and political importance. In his novel, Gaines explores the meaning of full manhood by encompassing the possibility of developing a whole, harmonious sense of belonging. Gaines positions his male characters against a cultural standard of behavior, exhibiting its false destructiveness. For example, there is the comparative case of Tee Bob and his father, Robert Samson. Robert has embraced an ideology affirming his superiority on the basis of gender, race, and wealth. His lack of reflection about the real consequences of this belief, however, results in his ultimate defeat. To uphold a system based on race he must exile the son who most resembles him. That Timmy has fought for his own integrity and in self-defense is, in Robert's mind, inconsequential in comparison to the challenge of his actions. Similarly, Robert must deny Tee Bob's expression of his love, again on the basis of race, for to acknowledge the feelings that clearly motivate his son would destroy any justification for the exploitation that has been ongoing. All the while Robert is shoring up this eroding levee, the flood waters of human nature eat away at its base. In Tee Bob's alignment with his mother, Mary Agnes, and Jane, he commands more respect than does his father. This respect, the novel suggests, is rooted in Tee Bob's inability to collude in the corrupt social system that imposes such strict and artificial standards of behavior on its members.

In fact, one could say that in all of the male characters associated with an admirable form of manhood, there clearly resides a spirit of self-sacrifice, a trait normally associated with females. Joe Pittman, Ned, Tee Bob, and Jimmy are all willing to die rather than conform to any preconceived standard of behavior. By making their own plans, they pose a direct threat to both conventional notions of manhood and race. Consequently, their deaths are expressions of integrity, not gestures of defeat.

Allied to the theme of manhood is the issue of brotherhood. One can look at the theme of brotherhood in its literal, narrow sense, but to do that would be to ignore the more comprehensive sense of human community. From the novel's beginning, we see human connections among people of both races as well as denials of responsibility. Exemplifying true brotherhood, Corporal Brown offers his sister's name to Jane, Big Laura provides leadership for the fleeing free people and defends Jane, and Jane assumes responsibility for Ned. On the other hand, there are those who blame the enslaved for the Civil War and the good "Christian" who can express only hatred. In Book III, "The Plantation," Gaines compresses the issue of brotherhood into the poignant tale of Timmy and Tee Bob.

Timmy and Tee Bob's relationship summarizes and presents the paradox of blood kinship in a culture that simultaneously values "family" even as it denies it. By choosing the most intimate and common instance that occurred on many southern plantations—the sexual appropriation of black women by white men—Gaines exposes the multiple hypocrisies and denials involved. Holding himself above any social criticism, Robert ties his horse in front of Verda's house, announcing his presence. Everyone, including his wife, knows and understands his reason for being there. His son by Verda inherits the looks, temperament, and gestures of his father. Still, in Robert's mind, Timmy is black, and thus not related to him. As he says to Amma Dean when he sends Timmy away, "There ain't no such thing as a half nigger" (146).

The price of Robert's denial of his link to Timmy is the ultimate dissolution of his own legacy. Much like Thomas Sutpen in Faulkner's *Ab-*

salom, Absalom!, Robert destroys the very goal of his existence: an heir to carry on his name and his way of life. In the end, there is no heir, and Robert's once supreme authority proves ineffectual against the moral authority of a frail, 110-year-old woman. Unlike Jane, Robert never acknowledges either his connection to the people on his land or his dependence on them. The tragedy here is not so much in Tee Bob's suicide but in the continuing denial of interdependence, of emotional and economic kinship.

Related to themes of manhood and brotherhood is that of the struggle of an entire race toward recognition and place. Gaines says that he had to do a good deal of historical research when he wrote this book. At the same time, he had to be very careful not to include detailed recall of dates or events because Miss Jane would hardly have access to that kind of information. Still, he wanted his title character to remain alert to signals of racial progress because he wished to submerge in her narrative a virtual history of African Americans. While analytical knowledge is unnecessary to comprehend the turn of events, knowing the general history will help readers to construct a chronology and mark significant changes. Some movement toward social acceptance is accurately reported through Jane's recalling athletic events broadcast over the radio such as the Louis/Schmeling boxing match of 1938; Jackie Robinson's appearance as the first black major league baseball player in 1947; Rosa Parks's defiance of custom on a Montgomery, Alabama, bus in 1956; or Authurene Lucy's brave attempt to integrate the University of Alabama in 1957. At other times, Jane will refer to specific events, including the violence that accompanied school integration in Alabama, Tennessee, and Arkansas in the late 1950s and the house bombings of civil rights workers Martin Luther King, Jr. and the Reverend Fred Shuttlesworth.

Binding these concerns is a spiritual theme, a theme Gaines presents in both its secular and religious forms. Throughout the novel, Jane notes—both in herself and others—an admirable stubborn spirit of perseverence. We see this, for example, in Jane's journey "north" with Ned, in Big Laura's fight to the death, and in Black Harriet's competitive nature, among others. All of these women demonstrate their value through direct action. But as the episode about Harriet illustrates, direct action can also lead to self-destruction, a lesson Jane eventually embraces.

On the heels of her tale of Harriet, Jane relates her religious "travels." The root of this word originates in the French "travail," meaning "to work," and the resulting religious convention asks that an individual tell her or his journey to redemption through Christ. Jane's journey is far from easy, reflecting the fact that her life until Ned's murder has contained more than enough difficulty. Still, after his death her religious struggles increase. Relocated at Samson, Jane seems surrounded by friends released from the burden of resentment through their religious commitment. When faith comes to Jane, she feels "like a big load just fell off my shoulders" (136). Her highly metaphoric account of her travels parallels her life's events as Ned, Joe, and Ned's murderer, Albert Cluveau, appear. Jane's struggle beyond their appeals and threats and her refusal to shift her burden to someone else win for her an emotional rebirth in which she feels "light and clean and good" (138). Relieved of remorse and resentment, her life moves forward with a renewed willingness to forgive.

Jane's religious conversion neither increases her humility nor makes her judgmental of others' actions. She seems to accept the example of Christ in its embracing form, suggesting a generosity of spirit lacking in more "respectable" church members like Just Thomas, who criticizes Jane for listening to baseball games and for arguing with him. This character may claim the moral high ground, but Jane's religious beliefs move beyond him. Instead of a pious, censorious form of religion, narrow in its views and critical of others, Jane's religion takes a typically flexible, sometimes disputatious and inclusive form, one leaving judgment to God.

In celebrating the spiritual strength of African Americans, Gaines realistically renders the role religion has played. At the same time, however, he doesn't credit the church with the power to change the social system. Just Thomas's expression of fear is both legitimate and typical, his resentment over being encouraged to risk personal safety suggestive of the church's initial reservations regarding political activism. More to the thematic point, however, may be the spiritual impetus moving characters like Jane, Ned, Joe, and Jimmy forward, an impetus undeterred by death as others assume the task of becoming part of human history.

A NEW HISTORICIST READING

New historicism is a critical lens attempting to focus a wide angle of vision. Beginning with the assumption that no text can be dealt with in isolation from its historical context, practitioners of this critical approach generally select from among many historical, psychological, socioeconomic, linguistic, and biographical frames of reference. Many practitioners will reveal in their analyses how an ideology—usually that of the ruling class—works to influence its readers. In general, new historicists look at history in much the same way Gaines's historian in *The Autobiography of Miss Jane Pittman* is forced to look at her story: not as a set of fixed facts proceeding in an orderly progression but rather as a discourse (or conversation) in need of interpretation. Further, most literary texts represent a diversity of differing voices, voices that speak for the power structure *and* voices expressive of other perspectives. History, then, cannot be used simply as a background for a text. Instead, it provides one of several possible beginning points of interchange between a creative work and other texts, institutions, even literary genres. A favorite word employed by new historicists to explain this interrelationship is "negotiation." In *The Autobiography of Miss Jane Pittman*, one can discover examples of such "negotiations," and thus it seems ideal for a new historicist approach.

From a biographical perspective, a critic might look closely at Gaines's life, recalling his Point Coupee childhood, especially the role his Aunt Augustine played in his life. Gaines has often recalled how she drew their small community to their home and how his life was shaped in part by the stories visitors shared. Other biographical parallels exist between the author's life and text—for example, Gaines's role, like Jimmy's, in reading and writing letters for people as well as the physical closeness of the community. These details, when added to such facts as Louisiana demographics, racial composition and ratio, average income, and educational opportunities provide deep background.

A new historicist might take into account not only the novel's inception but its reception as well. First published in 1971, *The Autobiography of Miss Jane Pittman* was issued in paperback the following year. Shortly thereafter, it was made into film for television and broadcast by CBS in 1974. To this day, it remains Gaines's most popular and best-known novel. Published on the heels of the civil rights struggles of the 1960s, *The Autobiography of Miss Jane Pittman* helped to explain why African Americans demanded recognition. Other writers had treated the struggle, but not as memorably as Gaines, whose timing, moreover, seemed perfect for a nation attemping to compensate for widely recognized and legally sanctioned racism. The film version not only helped popularize a relatively unknown writer, it also personalized a struggle in a touching dramatic performance. Instead of images of burning buildings and riots, Americans witnessed the humane and often humorous perspective of

Jane, brought to life by actress Cicely Tyson. For many viewers, impersonal resistence now had a name and a story they could embrace.

In writing this novel, Gaines's goal was to compose a "folk history," a point he makes clear in his use of the historian/editor he creates and in his blend of voices. Telling the story of a marginalized people, Gaines opens a discourse (negotiation) between those who have claimed to form culture (e.g., Robert Samson), and those who endure, perhaps prevail, within it (e.g., Jane). Jane's representative struggle for recognition, representation, and legal rights is a significant part of this novel. Interestingly, it's a historical tale that had rarely been voiced before the 1970s, particularly as a tale focusing on a group instead of an individual or events. Readers of *The Autobiography of Miss Jane Pittman* may not learn which Civil War battle led to a Confederate defeat in Louisiana, but they receive a vivid impression of the kinds of guerrilla tactics that terrorized people of color and forced them to submit to the *de facto* slavery system that persisted well into the twentieth century. The latter facts had generally been omitted from formal, traditional histories. Similarly, Gaines's folk history will not recount major events in the Civil Rights movement, such as passage of particular bills and Supreme Court decisions. Rather, his work will detail the extraordinarily common events of daily struggle. Told from the perspective of people who routinely deal with a civil and social system in which the unwritten and unspoken are more important than words on paper, this story constantly negotiates between the silent and the understood.

Another quite fascinating aspect of Gaines's novel is his use of radio and athletics as cultural markers. A new historicist might explore the relationship between history and popular culture, noting how the references to such cultural icons as Joe Louis and Jackie Robinson work to shape character and theme. Another approach would focus readers' attention on how specific figures come to represent social changes. Looking at history from the angle of popular culture instead of a more formalized historical perspective indicates how ordinary people "read" events.

Mixing large events with small, this novel suggests their elaborate similarities. While a civil rights historian might confirm the numerous factual events noted in the fiction, a new historicist will show how, from the perspective of millions of nameless victims and heroes, less politically significant events held equal importance. One might explore the intricacies of southern power politics, noting how poor whites and poor blacks are pitted against each other while others profit from this created antipathy. For example, the power behind Albert Cluveau, Ned's murderer, is acknowledged if unnamed. Cluveau is simply an instrument of sustained oppression. Jane will also counter historical accounts regarding Huey P. Long; most often dismissed by traditional histories as a southern demagogue, Long will be praised by Jane as an advocate for the impoverished. Whatever scandals historians may attribute to Long, and regardless of personal gossip tainted by racism, Jane asserts that Long is assassinated for his attempts to alter the social structure. After looking at such documented facts as the income of Louisiana residents in the 1920s and 1930s, the number of public schools, the average education of blacks and whites in the state, the length of the school year, and the primary industry, as well as other factors, a new historian might ask readers to consider how threatening the social changes advocated by Long were.

Over and over, *The Autobiography of Miss Jane Pittman* asks readers to negotiate between history and fiction, literary forms, representations of language, the unexpressed and the spoken, and among numbers of named characters whose voices merge to become a seemingly unified story. This text, placed in its various contexts, should provide a new historicist critic with a wealth of material from which to choose.

6

In My Father's House
(1978)

After his popular and critical success with *The Autobiography of Miss Jane Pittman*, Gaines quickly moved on to his next work. Ironically, this novel would present difficulties he never anticipated. In a 1991 interview, Gaines said that of all his novels to-date *In My Father's House* caused him the "greatest pain. It took me about seven years to write that book. I used every approach in the world to write that book" (Lowe, 248). Identifying the most frustrating areas as theme and character development, Gaines concluded that just about everything regarding this work gave him trouble; nevertheless, he felt he had to complete it, primarily because of its significant focus on what he calls the "father/son thing." Recognizing problematic relationships between absent fathers and injured sons as part of slavery's legacy, Gaines dramatizes a representative scenario. Though he addressed this idea indirectly in past works by using substitute father figures, Gaines this time focuses on blood relation.

If his fourth novel lacks the immediacy, vitality, comedy, and warmth of his previous work, it nevertheless compensates in part by focusing on two difficult and resonant themes: personal responsibility and the relation among past, present, and future. He dramatizes these ideas primarily through his main character, the Reverend Phillip J. Martin, a sixty-year-old Baptist minister and civil rights leader in St. Adrienne, Louisiana. Reaching for new levels of public recognition and leadership, Martin will literally and figuratively fall when a ghost from his past appears. This spectral figure turns out to be Martin's oldest son, whom he hasn't seen in over twenty years. Martin's efforts to reconcile his past with his present will result in his recognition of personal failure he has tried to bury.

STRUCTURE AND POINT OF VIEW

Gaines has said that one aim in writing this novel was to tell a story that resembles a Greek tragedy (Lowe, 184). The primary work defining tragedy remains Aristotle's *Poetics*, which describes tragedy as an imitation of nature reflecting "a high form of art exhibiting noble characters and noble deeds" (Bressler, 15). Aristotle further characterized tragedy as possessing form—that is, a beginning, middle, and end—with each of the parts relating to one another and all parts relating to the whole, resulting in what he called "organic unity." This unity extends to the tragic "hero," whose fall from power or position begins with an error or personal shortcoming rather than with evil intent. Through the hero's fall, the audience experiences a sort of emotional release or cleansing, which Aristotle called "catharsis." Aristotle further found tragedy to express the universal, not the particular; thus, tragedy deals with ideas and emotions common to all. Moreover, tragedy does not concern itself primarily with what has happened. That is the job of history. Instead, tragedy concentrates on what *could* happen. Although Gaines has never stated directly just what he means by Greek tragedy, it's clear that what he wanted in this novel was to have one character representing the whole, and he wanted the hero's actions to dramatize the timeless classical themes of the degree of personal responsibility and the relationship of past to present. Frank Shelton has observed the novel's classical lines in its focus on the issues of determinism and free will as well as the consequences of inordinate pride (Shelton, "Ernest Gaines After Jane Pittman," 343). Another classical element at work in this novel is found in the echoes of Sophocles's play *Oedipus the King*. Readers will not find similar patterns of dramatic action but rather thematic echoes in the hero's efforts to avoid his past, the son's mission to "kill" his father, and a rather unhealthy relationship between mother and son.

When we first see Gaines's protagonist, the Reverend Martin, he stands at the height of social position in St. Adrienne, Louisiana. Minister of the Solid Rock Baptist Church and a civil rights leader, Martin has both a firm base, as the name of his church suggests, and a psychological link to the Reverend Martin Luther King, Jr., as indicated by his name. Large, handsome, and prosperous, Martin commands respect by black and white members of the community. He is their "King Martin" (30). However, Martin has not always enjoyed this high degree of prominence and respect. His actions of the past fifteen years have been an effort to compensate for past wrongs, including a dissolute lifestyle and refusal to recognize and support a family he has fathered. Twenty years later, a ghost from his past returns to St. Adrienne, and Phillip Martin, like all tragic heroes, has to fall.

The novel opens with the appearance of a mysterious young man calling himself Robert X, and the first few chapters pose questions about his presence in the community: Who is he? Where did he come from? Why is he in St. Adrienne? The character's oblique answers—when he bothers to answer questions at all—fail to satisfy anyone. Silent, scrawny, unkempt, and withdrawn, Robert X shows interest only in the identity of Martin, and his questions stir community commentary. In the role of a Greek chorus, other characters in the novel will sketch Martin's character. But Robert X challenges them by wondering, "Do you ever know a man's character?" (16). Thus, the first section of the novel begins to raise questions about the basics of character and leadership, dramatizing a division in community leadership, and reflecting a high degree of disillusionment among young teachers regarding issues of leadership and social progress. Finally, at the end of the first section, Gaines emphasizes his hero's tragic fall by having Martin literally fall to the floor when he first recognizes his son across the room.

The middle section of the book focuses on Martin's struggle to hold back his past. After fifteen years of difficult, often dangerous civil rights work, he now believes he has earned his prominence. Since the community has elevated him, holding him as a model leader, Martin is understandably reluctant to make his dilemma public. In fact, he will not share the news that his eldest son has appeared even with his wife, Alma, or one of his longtime supporters, Howard Mills (a man who knows Martin's past very well). Instead, Martin begins an exploration into his past, a past he has successfully blocked from his present. This journey will appropriately return him to Reno Plantation and to Baton Rouge, where he spent his young manhood. Comprising the majority of the novel, this section includes Martin's actual claim of his son, his subsequent fall from political power, and his struggle to reconcile his past with his present. Trying to recall his son's name without speaking of his own deficiency, Martin embarks on a night journey of his soul.

The resolution of the novel occurs appropriately in chapter 11, with Martin learning the whole story of his first family's dissolution, primarily caused by his failure as a husband and father. Having recognized his guilty past, Martin now believes his entire life has been for nothing. Beaten down with despair, he decides that he has no future. But a young woman, Beverly Ricord, helps Martin to see the value of his life, not only by revealing the difference his presence has made in her life but also by pointing toward the gains he led others in making. Reminding Martin of his second son, Patrick, Beverly helps him to see the difference his participation in his family's life—and his community's life—can make. Suggestive of both a second chance and the future, Patrick now becomes the measure of Martin's success. This novel concludes on a somber but positive note, with Martin and Alma acknowledging the need to "start again" (214).

In his struggle to write *In My Father's House*, Gaines experimented with narrative voice, ultimately settling on third-person omniscient point of view because no one character, certainly not his protagonist, could plausibly tell this story. Realizing that he lacks the control with this narrative perspective that he usually enjoys, Gaines labored over the representation of a character who "keeps too much inside" (Lowe, 89), and thus refuses to reveal his thoughts and feelings with other characters. This results in a breach between reader and protagonist, a breach uncharacteristic of Gaines's best work. In his best fiction, language reveals character. But this particular character uses language—more specifically the avoidance of language or indirection—as a shield, presenting a barrier between past and present. Other characters must step in and fulfill the mission of drawing Martin's character. But because they have limited knowledge of him, their presentation seems scattered. While the apparently fugitive and fragmented characterization of Martin is thematically appropriate, its dramatic objectivity holds readers at such a remove that he never assumes the full life of Gaines's most memorable protagonists.

PLOT DEVELOPMENT

Gaines begins this novel with a mystery: Who is this bedraggled young man? Why has he come to St. Adrienne? What does he plan to do? What has happened to make him the way he is? The issue of *what* happens is important because it makes up what is called "story." But *why* events occur falls into the category of plot. Driving the plot is this question:

what is Robert's function and why does he have the effect on characters that he has? This character—an apparent stranger making no claims upon the community—begins the sequence of events that comprise the novel. Though no one wants to embrace his presence, there nevertheless remains a nagging sense of human obligation. This paradoxical reticence and guilt is best voiced by Robert's reluctant landlady, Virginia Colar. Despite her reservations over having Robert as a lodger, she accepts him, saying to herself, "where else could he go?" (4). Robert reminds other characters of their marginal social status, his very name suggestive of his refusal to accept any prescribed social position.

Having introduced a mystery figure, Gaines proceeds to link him to the protagonist, apparently unaware of Robert's existence and unassailable from such a marginalized character. Robert's focus on Martin, however, directs reader attention, not simply to Martin's public appearance but to something buried in his past. So the question of *why* shifts to Martin. Who is this puzzling character? What connects Robert to Martin? How will Martin react to this character? What changes will occur? Robert stirs community conversation, his character serving as a catalyst in community discussions of leadership and purpose. In fact, Gaines moves his story forward primarily through a series of meetings and conversations: Virginia Colar with Robert, Elijah Green with Robert, the schoolteachers at the Congo Room, the civil rights committee at Martin's house, Martin with Sheriff Nolan, Martin with Robert, then Martin with people from his past life. These dramatic scenes reveal character and build theme. If this device seems worn at times, it nevertheless addresses the complexity of Gaines's thematic intentions. While moving forward in chronological time during a two-week time span, Martin returns to places that help him recover his past, and he moves back to characters who can fill his considerable lapses of memory. Ideally, a novel achieves a fine balance between plot and thematic development, making the ideas more felt than articulated. Given the weight and complexity of the ideas Gaines dramatizes in this novel, readers might better address questions of thematic development simultaneously with plot development.

CHARACTERIZATION

Martin's son, calling himself Robert X, is characterized more as a haunting spirit than a substantial fictional presence. Thin, silent, obscure, and shabby, he appropriately wanders, signifying a restlessness of spirit and a lack of place. Gaines evokes both his denial of his father and a certain revolutionary ambiance with Robert's addition of an "X." Recalling Malcolm X, who said that the X represented the unknown African ancestor instead of a name conferred by a slave owner, the X also suggests Robert's unclaimed status. Since Martin never married Johanna Ricord, despite fathering her three children, his children are considered "bastards" by society. Denied the legitimacy conferred by his father's name, Robert, whose given name is Etienne, makes up his own identity, however meager. While Robert's character will have dramatic impact, his primary purpose is to create a sense of mystery. His silence and cryptic remarks serve to awaken community awareness and sharpen thematic conflicts. Robert's emotional distress is written in his every movement. He confesses to Shepherd that his soul "don't feel good" (25). Where his father believes himself to be a sturdy object like a tree, Robert identifies with garbage: "broke glass, tin cans. Any trash" (25). An empty vessel at best, Robert sees himself as both broken and discarded. He blames Martin for emasculating him and destroying his family. This hopeless character will speak his piece and disappear like the haunting spirit he is.

Readers may find Gaines's main character even more difficult to grasp. A man who shares personal feelings with no one—not even his wife— the Martin other characters see is the same one readers see: a public mask crafted to convey an image of confidence, prosperity, and solidity. Indeed, Martin's external features are so persuasive that his sudden collapse has far more impact than it might ordinarily have. Like his church's name, Martin believes himself to be the community's "solid rock." As the foundation for social change in St. Adrienne, Martin hopes to build an illustrious future in a greater public arena as a U.S. congressman. Aware of the importance of appearance, Martin will work to maintain the illusion of substantial citizen. Thus, he will lie to his wife and friends, sneak around in his own home, and ultimately betray the faith his community has placed in him by making a private arrangement with Sheriff Nolan to keep his past quiet.

Readers are given a glimpse of Martin's interior life through a dream he recalls in chapter 5. This fragmentary memory of his last transaction with his oldest son twenty-two years earlier suggests Martin's regret and his change, for the dream figure is kinder to both his son and his lover than the actual Martin. Believing this dream prescient, Martin will initially feel more regret than understanding. Identifying with a lone pecan tree across the street from his home, Martin turns to God for solace. His choice of sermon text supports the father/son theme and further suggests that he has been thinking about his son subconsciously. The text from John 14 provides the novel's title. Focusing on forgiveness, understanding, leadership, and sacrifice, it features Christ, shortly before his crucifixion, explaining his role to his disciples. Gaines plays on the meaning, contrasting Christ's acceptance of his sacrifice to make room for others and Martin's inability to make room for his son in his life, his home. Indeed, it's reasonable to assume that Martin has chosen this passage of Christ going in advance to make room for his followers so that Martin's own followers will see a similarity between Christ and himself. Casting himself as an obedient sacrificial figure for a greater good and as a leader, Martin wants to believe that his public actions will atone for his private failures. But if his future effectiveness is compromised by his past deficiency, how can he compensate?

Most of the character development will take place through action, as Martin moves back in time and place to recover his past. Failing to reach his son during their single conversation, Martin will return to where everything began, Reno Plantation. His starting point appropriately is his godmother Angelina Bouie, responsible for his spiritual upbringing. But he cannot confess his inability to remember his son's name when he faces Angelina, though she is perceptive enough to know "Something ain't right" (110). She will, however, give Martin the key to his past by telling him that Chippo, an old friend, has recently returned to Reno with news of Johanna. Martin will continue to move through stages of recognition until he discovers the cause of his emotional paralysis. Gaines links the relationships between fathers and sons to the issue of political action through a series of conversations. Of particular importance are those with Reverend Peters and Billy, a Vietnam veteran. Peters clearly represents the conservative approach of gradual change and acceptance. He believes that faith in God is enough, that prayer and faith will ultimately right every wrong. So focused is he on God as a solution to every human problem, Peters cannot see the generational gap Martin points out: "There's a gap between us and our sons . . . that even He . . . can't seem to close" (154). Peters's denial of any gap sounds more formulaic than credible, especially given the series of rootless young men brought to Martin's attention. Billy, however, helps Martin to see one possible consequence of this gap.

Gaines creates Billy as Robert X's active twin. Both characters are small and thin. Where Robert wears an army cap, Billy dresses in an army field jacket. Robert's scars are invisible; Billy's visible scar attracts attention. Unlike Robert, who commits suicide in his despair, however, Billy elects to fight back. He is the leader and primary recruiter for a guerrilla army training to attack "the last crutch for Western Civilization" in order to "put the world back right" (162). Billy's rejection of integrationist philosophy, his lack of faith in any course of action short of mass destruction shocks Martin. Can Billy not see any social changes that so many have worked for? Trying to get to the root of Billy's motivation, Martin asks whether Billy has children and then about Billy's relationship with his father. When Billy characterizes his "average" relationship with his father as "I don't bother him, he don't bother me" (165), Martin wonders whether or not men are born with this gap. Religion is not a solution to this problem, according to Billy, because the church offers "more separation" (166). And the Civil Rights movement did nothing to close the distance between black fathers and sons. As for bridging his personal gap with his father, Billy says, "My daddy got to catch up with me" because Billy refuses to "go back where he's at" (166). Billy's character will help Martin understand how the younger generation feels about "God, Law, and Country" (170). Martin will leave Billy, wondering just how to reach the next generation.

Gaines will give speaking roles to many characters, most of them male. But the female characters serve a special purpose in this book. Their marginal status will underscore community fragmentation, and their voicelessness will emphasize an essential deficiency in community discussion over direction. Essentially, there are five small but key women's roles in this novel. Angelina Bouie provides essential information and insight into Martin's character. While critic Frank Shelton maintains that Martin's distant relationship with his godmother suggests a movement away from his origins, Angelina's language suggests that she knows him better than he knows himself (Shelton, "After Jane Pittman," 343). Though she has had limited contact with Martin, she nevertheless provides a significant gateway to his past. As for Martin's wife, Alma, she seems in danger of being ignored. Indeed, Martin actually tries to leave her out of his emotional life altogether. Alma's understanding is explicit, however, in her saying to him, "I want you to come to me sometime" (71). Martin understands this only as a sexual invitation, but Alma means spiritual intimacy, a sharing of feelings. Alma, whose name means soul, may loosen her grasp of Martin, but her intention is to grant him the freedom he needs to find himself. In the end, she searches for him and supports him, promising a new beginning together. Alma's pride and faith in Martin are ultimately reiterated by Beverly Ricord. By pointing out how Martin's past has influenced his actions, she helps him to reconcile past to present, to gain what Valerie Babb calls a "spiritual understanding" of his past actions and motivations (110). In their perhaps stereotypical roles as nurturers, Gaines's women characters nevertheless serve key roles. Their loyalty, faith, understanding, and forgiveness are significant factors in Martin's success and in their future.

Two women from Martin's past appear in this book, Johanna Rey and Adeline Toussaint. Like Robert X and Billy, these characters mirror one another. Johanna, Martin's first lover, allows herself to be a victim of his selfishness. She invests her emotional life in this man, confusing their physical intimacy with an emotional one. When Martin fails to claim his family through marriage, Johanna leaves, hoping that Martin will follow her. But her physical remove simplifies Martin's desire to forget. While Johanna lives her life waiting for him to appear, Martin will succeed in entirely blocking their existence from his memory. The damage Johanna inflicts on their children, especially her oldest son, by making him "the man of the house" is unconscious, although asking any five-year-old to assume an adult's role is clearly unreasonable, the action of a dependent individual. In contrast to Johanna's long-standing loyalty and emotional suffering is Adeline Toussaint's emotional independence. Described in physically attractive terms, Adeline exerts the same sexual magnetism for Phillip Martin that she had fifteen years earlier, when they were lovers. Encountering her late in the novel, Martin is shocked by her amused statement that she was only pretending to love him. Her revelation that she could enjoy physical intimacy without emotional connection pierces Martin's ego, for although he has cast away numbers of women, he never imagined himself in a similar position. Adeline makes Martin own up to his own lack of emotional commitment, forcing him to see himself in an entirely new and rather unflattering light as someone she uses.

THEMATIC CONCERNS AND LITERARY DEVICES

Implicit in the father/son relationship are issues of leadership, change, the role of the past, and personal responsibility. All of these major ideas are represented by Robert X and Phillip Martin. Robert's unexpected appearance in Phillip Martin's life comes at a critical time, when the community is considering sending Martin to Washington, D.C., as a representative. So the issue of leadership occurs, along with the question of fitness. These are perennial political issues, and particularly significant in this work because of time and place, or the setting.

The setting of the novel is Gaines's South in the early 1970s, after the assassinations of Martin Luther King, Jr., John F. Kennedy, and Robert Kennedy. Their images hang on the wall of Martin's study, partially as support for Martin's integrationist views. King's image, flanked by those of the Kennedy brothers, also suggests a certain dependence upon influential whites for social gains. This physical grouping is repeated in a description of Martin as "the big man talking to the white folks" (32) and in Martin's position between Octave Bacheron and Anthony McVey after his literal fall. A second portrait, "hanging evenly" with the first, offers a different configuration. Featuring images of Abraham Lincoln, Booker T. Washington, and Frederick Douglass, all of whom overcame personal obstacles to achieve success, this second montage supports an idea of self-help. Various conversations throughout Gaines's novel will reiterate an ideological split over how to make additional social gains after the limited success of the 1960s Civil Rights movement. What we hear and see during the party at Martin's house focuses on leadership, especially the degree of white participation in the Civil Rights movement. With the original leaders aging and young people disenchanted over limited gains in social justice, questions of direction arise. Martin clearly follows the example of King. His past actions and planned protest of Chenal's discriminatory hiring and wages recall King's practice of protest and boycott, and his message of "love," "understanding," and "persistence" (37) is an echo of King's nonviolent ideology. The young teachers at the Congo Room, however, believe these actions useless. Whatever gains in social progress were effected through protest are at an end. One young man declares that demonstrations and boycotts are "over with." He continues, "Them honkies gave up some, because of conscience, because of God. But they ain't giving up no more" (21).

Most of the young adults in this novel will express reservations about social direction. Having come up against the limits of legal changes, they continue to experience profound social inequities. At this point, they cannot decide on who should lead or in which direction to move. Beverly Ricord says that the teachers should "be the ones out there in front," but her opinion does not receive serious consideration (21). Other possible directions are explicit in Robert's surname choice. When Virginia Colar first hears Robert's last name as "X," she struggles to recall which group he might belong to, Black Panthers or Black Muslims. At the risk of oversimplification, it's fair to say that the former group believed that violence was justified in bringing about racial justice while the latter advocated a form of separation. Readers can hear an echo of the Black Panthers in the voice of Billy, who supports violent revolution as a solution to racism, claiming that "Nothing changed" (169). Looking into the disillusioned faces of the young he meets, Martin sees his neglected son and the chasm of understanding he helped to create.

Gaines's choice of the father/son theme has particular resonance for Americans of African descent for obvious historical reasons. Claiming a past inevitably linked to slavery remains shameful to some and, at the very least, uncomfortable to others. Many have tried to ignore or forget a history scarred by slavery while others have used slavery's heritage as an excuse for personal failings. Toni Morrison's *Beloved* deals specifically with the difficulty characters have in reconciling past to present. Her characters have much in common with Phillip Martin in refusing to think their past has ramifications for their present. But the past has a way of making its presence felt, and when it literally fells Martin, he is forced to reclaim a history he has tried to obliterate. For Martin, the past is useful only as an excuse as he attempts to justify his treatment of his first family to Robert, initially by blaming the world and then by blaming history. Gaines, however, rejects the stigma of slavery as an excuse for a lack of commitment to family, though he understands the relationship of past to present. He will force his character to recover the past, for without the past, there can be no future.

Martin has put his past behind him, believing that his religious conversion has absolved him of past wrongs. Even his subconscious has revised his early character, as we see when Martin compares his prescient dream of his son and Johanna to the brutal reality of the past. He has believed that by placing himself in danger, by assuming a leading role in creating social justice, he not only compensates for but entirely relinquishes his past. Robert's reappearance, however, reminds Martin of aftereffects. When Martin links an unidentified corpse he reads about in the newspaper to Robert X, he recognizes his son's unclaimed state. Still hoping to keep his son's reappearance private, he goes to Sheriff Nolan, hoping that money will purchase a discreet release. But the price Nolan demands for Robert's release will cost Martin the leadership of his committee because Nolan asks that Martin place his individual desires above the interests of all. Refusing to release Robert without Martin's promise to call off the planned protest demonstration against Albert

Chenal, Nolan shows Martin that he is not as pure as he believes himself to be. Nolan ends their negotiation saying, "I always thought you was different. . . . Just go to show how wrong a man can be" (92).

At this point, Martin believes that he can still explain and defend his past. Realizing that his son has no interest in what he has to say, he nevertheless tries to account for his actions in their only conversation. Appropriately, this takes place outside St. Adrienne, in Martin's car, with no witnesses. Having failed to spark conversation a number of times, Martin finally squeezes an answer from his son by asking about Johanna. The story he hears, however, is one he's unprepared to deal with, for it branches from Martin's refusal to care for his family, a refusal constantly reiterated to readers by Martin's inability to recall his son's given name. Robert says that he has returned to kill Martin for "destroying the family" (99), and proceeds to horrify Martin with an account of his emotional destruction. After Martin's refusal of paternal responsibility, Johanna makes her oldest son the "man of the house," his primary job being, apparently, to protect his mother and sister. Then, while she still loves Martin and hopes that he will appear to claim his family, Johanna takes on a series of temporary lovers, the last of whom rapes her daughter Justine. This crisis results in a violent disagreement between Martin's sons. Etienne, the eldest, wants the law to handle the problem while Antoine wants to shoot the rapist. Antoine carries out his revenge, is arrested, tried, and convicted to five years. Believing himself betrayed by his father and by God, Etienne feels emasculated and alone. Instead of blaming history, he blames his absent father, whose denial of paternal responsibility has resulted in this tragedy. The link between father and law is clear in Robert's question, "Why should the law protect us when the father won't?" (103). Having made his point, Robert walks away from his father, his parting words declaring that he doesn't need anything from his father any longer—neither his name nor his feeble justifications. His refusal to wait for a response emphasizes his rootlessness, emotional estrangement, and impatience.

After failing to justify his past acts to his son, Martin must now face those he leads. Returning home, he discovers committee members who have found out that their leader has placed his personal concerns above everyone. In agreeing not to protest against Chenal, Martin has effectively sold out the movement. To committee members, his decision undermines the unity that has been so important to both survival and success. When Martin justifies his decision, Mills is quick to point out that everyone has sons and the goal of their work is "so our boys will come back home" (125). Martin's purely self-serving decision, then, makes him "unfit" for leadership, because, as Howard Mills says, "If you had come out in the open and told people who that boy was, none of this never wouda happened" (129). Instead, trying to maintain an illusion of solidity, Martin has betrayed not simply his family but his community and church. Stripped of his authority, Martin is ironically cut adrift to explore why his son has returned. He leaves for Baton Rouge in search of his friend, Chippo.

Unlike Martin, Chippo has never turned his back on his past. In fact, we will learn that Chippo is the same as he always was, still continuing a life of drinking, gambling, womanizing, and wandering. As Martin tracks Chippo through the bars, gambling houses, black neighborhoods, and surroundings of Baton Rouge, he will literally embark on a night journey of the soul. This literal and metaphoric movement is a well-known literary archetype suggesting a desire for discovery and change. The night journey in particular often represents a character's descent into the unconscious. With each new location, Phillip Martin will cross a new threshold of recognition. Each of these encounters will remove a layer of self-protection until, in the end, Martin can ask a fundamental question: "When will we make our legs go to our sons and make our arms protect our sons?" (202).

Dealing with such complex personal and ideological issues forced Gaines to draw on more conventional literary devices than is typical of his previous work. In what is possibly his most consciously *literary* novel, Gaines draws upon two main archetypes. This term refers to primary images or pattern shaped by human experience from earliest times. The journey is one such pattern, for example, that has been used by many cultures to convey a coming of awareness or education of a character. Gaines's use of the night journey has already been mentioned, as one especially focused on psychological awareness. And, clearly, Gaines employs this image as a plot pattern, when, in chapter 9, Martin travels to Baton Rouge. The journey routinely has the protagonist encounter representative figures who increase understanding. During this long night, Martin will first encounter two women who tell him of a Vietnam veteran's murder, an incident conveying just how the Civil Rights movement has failed to address fully such profound human wrong. As Martin drives through black neighborhoods, he will see and hear about children without fathers, a recognition that forces him to reflect first upon his failure to his present family and then to his unclaimed children by other women. Once a source of male pride, these unacknowledged children now cause Martin to wonder about himself and his absent role in their lives. In his conversation with Reverend Peters, Martin will ask, "Where was Turner?" This refers to the failure of the veteran's father to provide for and protect his family. In every successive episode, Martin will link dead young men to absent fathers.

A father's sacrifice of his son is another familiar literary pattern. Many readers can trace this archetypal pattern back to the Bible, where Abraham agrees to sacrifice his son Isaac and God sacrifices Christ. These dramatic episodes evoke a host of complex human issues, including power, obedience, understanding, and faith. Gaines has Martin link Robert to Christ by saying that he blames himself for denying him (Robert) twice (58), and by having Martin face a picture of the crucifixion, this time asking "Why?" instead of repeating his usual prayer (69). Martin's choice of sermon text, offering Christ's understanding and acceptance of his coming sacrifice, however, is in stark contrast with Robert's refusal to accept any of his father's reasons for sacrificing him. Robert, the unclaimed body frozen in a ditch, the murdered Vietnam veteran, Turner, and Billy all appear in this novel to illustrate the dire consequences of unrecognized and unreconciled sons.

One of the most frequently occuring features of the journey motif is naming, which involves knowing what something is and calling it by its proper name. Martin's inability to recall his son's name literally drives him to recover his past. As long as Robert is anonymous, he has no reality for Martin. Once he sees Robert and hears his name, however, something strikes Martin as "wrong," and he will try in vain to remember what he called his son. Martin's initial measures are to claim relationship in reference to himself only. Thus, he will say "my son" to Howard Mills and Sheriff Nolan, his language reflective of his self-centeredness and ignorance of his son. Even during their conversation, Martin wants to explain himself to Robert more than to know his son, as indicated again by his reluctance to ask his name. Only at the very end of the novel, having listened to Chippo's account of his family's suffering, does Martin, in a rush of recognition, call his son by both first and last names, Etienne Martin.

Appropriately, this tragic tale takes place during winter. Gaines uses weather to unify and to set the mood of his novel. Throughout the novel's action, the weather remains steadfastly cold, wet, and gray. The temperature seems only to drop lower and lower, adding to the physical discomfort of the characters. This raw weather sets the novel's bleak tone, and reflects Martin's psychological state. Along with the weather,

Gaines will employ other suggestive images. As already mentioned, Robert's association of himself with trash is revealing of someone who sees himself not merely as discarded but broken as well. Early in the novel, Robert will tell Shepherd that he is just out of prison. Later, readers will actually learn that this "prison" is a self-imposed punishment as Etienne retreats to his room in Johanna's apartment after his brother, Antoine, refuses to recognize him. Chippo will describe this room as a "crypt," suggesting Etienne's burial and his premature emotional death. These images contrast sharply with that of the pecan tree symbolizing Phillip Martin. Though alone and stripped by the season, this image, so deeply rooted in the soil, conveys a sense of stature and strength.

Gaines also draws readers' attention to physical appearance. Having created a main character unable to reveal his interior life, Gaines must give some preparatory signals to aid the understanding of readers. He draws a sharp contrast between Robert's initial thin appearance and Martin's substantial one. This will change during Martin's journey, as he begins to recognize his past actions for what they were. Martin becomes increasingly haggard, recalling Robert's desolate state. In the end, he will feel the full burden of his past weighing on him, a burden he refuses to shift to another. In fact, this threatens to topple Martin back into his past life until Gaines arranges his rescue by Chippo, Beverly, and Alma. Their need for Martin's example and faith in his leadership promise to restore him to public action, but it will be a much changed character, one who now fully feels a father's obligation to his sons.

A PSYCHOLOGICAL READING

Given the classical structure of *In My Father's House*, with its emphasis upon the main character's repressed past and its consequences, a psychological analysis of the novel seems inescapable. Psychological criticism begins with Sigmund Freud, the father of psychoanalysis. Freud's theory of how human minds work appears in *The Interpretation of Dreams* (1900). Dividing the mind into three parts—the ego, the superego, and the id—Freud went on to distinguish their particular functions. The ego is the conscious, rational function of the brain, and the id is its opposite, a complex of irrational, passionate drives rarely sanctioned by polite society. The superego acts as a negotiant between these extremes, often working with the ego to repress the id's powerful urges. A balance among these parts is rare, partly because the id is so strong that it invariably leaks through in such disguised forms as dreams, language, and creative activity. Freud's theory focused on using dreams as a means of understanding the unconscious, an important discovery for everyone because it's through the interplay of the conscious and unconscious that we create ourselves and our world (Bressler, 80).

While Freud laid the foundation, subsequent followers chose to branch off from his theories, and their theories have also proven fruitful to literary discussions. Carl Jung, one of Freud's students who became a physician and psychiatrist, employed some of Freud's ideas and rejected others. His three-part division of the human psyche included the conscious, the personal unconscious and the "collective unconscious," a phrase Jung coined to describe a kind of unconscious memory transmitted through generations and appearing in archetypes. He defined archetypes as universally shared human experiences, such as birth and death, which appear in stories and dreams (Bressler, 92). In the 1950s, Canadian literary theorist Northrup Frye would develop archetypal criticism based on Jung's theory. Because psychoanalytic criticism can so easily compliment other critical approaches, the psychoanalytical approach promises to continue as a viable method of literary interpretation.

Martin's avoidance of his past provides wide space for psychological investigation. After recognizing his son, Martin is confined to his bed. Significantly, he doesn't want to think of his son while in this intimate space; Martin can think only in his office. His division between the unconscious and reason, then, seems clear. Indeed, these self-imposed walls between conscious and unconscious, past and present are precisely the source of Martin's trouble. Initially, Martin wants only to "make sense" of what has happened instead of clearly seeing his role (47). Thinking of his son, Martin recalls a dream which he characterizes as "a warning," but a dream that says much about his past and present character (50).

In his dream, Martin recalls his last transaction with his son twenty-two years earlier. Acting as a go-between, Martin's son, Etienne, is sent by Johanna to alert Martin of their departure. The woman with whom Martin is sleeping gives the boy three dollars, and Johanna returns the money. Martin's dream clearly reflects guilt over his past actions, for in his dream he goes after his son instead of waiting for him to leave, and he returns the money to the woman instead of burning the money and beating her, as he had actually done. Martin's dream also reveals that however deeply he has buried his past actions, they will surface. It forces him to consider Johanna, not in any conscious way, but rather through imagery. Martin notes that while Johanna favored wearing bright colors—especially yellow—in reality, she is dressed in black in his dream, suggestive of mourning. Refusing to dwell on the significance of his dream, Martin will note his regret and hope that he would act differently now. But elements revelatory of character present themselves in this dream, elements a psychological critic would develop.

Martin focuses on the "small hands" and "small arms" of his son, their size reflective of age and inability. His dream reveals the full extent of his guilt by telling readers that he neither provides money nor acts in any way to contact his son. When he acts, having waited until his family has left, Martin will brutalize the woman who provided the money. He will recall Etienne's parting gesture of reaching toward him in need and welcome, seeing in hindsight how much his son needed him, but he cannot see his son's face or remember his name, both reflective of inattention. By contrast, his other two children remain oblivious to his presence, a memory suggestive of his utter absence in their lives.

Just how Martin brings his past to a conscious level is detailed in his movements back to Reno Plantation and Baton Rouge. The symbolic resonance of night is particularly important. Writers as early as the Greeks associated night with the unconscious, believing that darkness preceded light (creation). Thus, night becomes especially representative of potentiality because it anticipates day, just as light often signifies knowledge. For Carl Jung, the night journey was a descent into the unconscious, an exploration of another side of life that mysteriously affects consciousness. Jung believed that a convergence of conscious and unconscious at the journey's end would result in a form of rebirth (Cirlot, 229).

Gaines multiplies images of the unconscious beginning in chapter 9, when Martin crosses the Mississippi River driving into Baton Rouge. In fact, Martin will cross water twice more in his restless attempt to find Chippo. Water is often seen as another medium between unconscious and conscious, life and death. A third signifier of Martin's unconscious is evoked by the dark, narrow labyrinthine streets of Chippo's neighborhood. As he negotiates these streets, literally asking the way, Martin's thoughts will constantly return to his family: how will he explain; how will he compensate for his failure? Instead of the confident public man with answers of chapter 1, Martin becomes a character reaching toward fundamental questions: "He wondered if he knew his people and if he could do anything to help" (147). Everywhere he looks, Martin sees his absence mirrored in family life. In moving back, Martin bridges past with present, facing what he truly was and seeing the effects. Thus, he finds a balance between conscious and unconscious.

Along with these archetypal images, Gaines provides a siren in the person of Adeline Toussaint. Sirens are also archetypal figures whose purpose is to tempt heroes, to deter them from their mission (Cirlot, 297). Adeline, like a siren, has a dual purpose. Initially, she forces Martin to own up to his own lack of emotional investment in his relations with women, and then she makes him feel used when she tells him that she could enjoy physical intimacy without any emotional investment. This is as close as Martin, a womanizer for most of his life, will come to understanding what Johanna must have felt in being rejected. Throughout their conversation, Martin experiences feelings he knows "aren't right" (175), and though he refuses Adeline's offer of her favors at the Red Top, he reconsiders after learning of Etienne's suicide. Here, Adeline provides the final obstacle between Martin and his mission, for in going to her, he would fall from the path leading to understanding and acceptance. Chippo, more than any other character, sees the significance of Adeline and refuses to let Martin go to her. Saying that he needs Martin to care for everyone and as a person to look up to, Chippo voices the needs of the community before turning to Shepherd, representing the next generation, for additional support.

Instead of Shepherd's providing additional reasons why Phillip Martin should continue as a community leader, the deciding reasons are provided by Beverly Ricord. Martin wants this young woman to understand who he was before she even speaks. Characterizing himself to Beverly as "an animal . . . who took everything [he] could from [his] fellow man," Martin believes that God somehow "owes" him his son, Etienne, as a reward for his awareness and sacrifices of the past fifteen years (210). His public confession stands in contrast with his silence of the first scenes in the novel; Martin's humility and outpouring of feeling suggest a substantial change in his character. Beverly leads Martin to see that acknowledging the past is a necessary step, not an end in itself. To her, the past is a step toward the future, and she skillfully changes the direction of Martin's focus from Etienne to Patrick, his young son by Alma: "We work toward the future. To keep Patrick from going to that trestle" (213). She then directs Martin to Chippo's bedroom where Alma rests.

The novel's conclusion appropriately takes place here, where Phillip Martin finally admits to his wife that he is "lost." No psychological critic would fail to note the significance of setting, Martin's physical position, or Alma's final words, for they all work together to signify not only the final and essential recognition by Martin of his state but also a rebirth of a new man. Readers should note the word "lost," with its biblical echo of being lost before being found. Significantly, though, the final words of the novel are given to Alma, who silences Martin's expression of despair with a simple yet firm affirmation of starting again. Alma's use of the plural pronoun "We" indicates their effort will be collective instead of individual.

A psychological analysis of this novel adds insight to the characters, to the implications of particular images and settings, and enhances the novel's classical structure. As a singular theoretical lens, a psychological approach would fail to explain the complex historical and political issues Gaines means for readers to see. But used in conjunction with other lenses, this approach helps readers to see the character behind the mask, the timelessness behind the contemporary, the perennial human struggle to understand place and purpose.

7

A Gathering of Old Men
(1983)

If *The Autobiography of Miss Jane Pittman* ends by signaling the beginning of a social revolution, *A Gathering of Old Men* brings this conflict to a logical conclusion. Set in 1979 on the Marshall Plantation, Gaines's fifth novel focuses on a group of elderly men who come to terms with their regret over past passivity and decide to claim their manhood and dignity. The action begins when Candy Marshall, part owner of the plantation, calls a child to deliver several messages. Men are to come with twelve-gauge shotguns and number-five shells to Mathu's house. Candy believes that Mathu, a black man who has helped raise her, has shot Beau Boutan, a Cajun farmer who has leased the Marshall Plantation. Trying to protect Mathu, Candy plans to confess to the murder, and she hopes others will claim guilt in order to obscure Mathu's culpability. Long recognized for his clear sense of manhood and refusal to submit to white men, Mathu is certain to be arrested by Sheriff Mapes. Candy— and everyone else in the story—also fears reprisals by the Boutan family, known for its cruelty to blacks. Once men of the surrounding area hear Candy's message, they consider their past and decide to take advantage of an opportunity to stand and be recognized as men. Mainly in their seventies, these characters seem an odd collection of defenders, but during the course of a day, most claim their position as men and earn respect from Sheriff Mapes.

STRUCTURE AND POINT OF VIEW

This novel's structure is almost classical in its attention to the unities of time, place, and action. Setting his work on a south Louisiana plantation in 1979 and having the action take place during an eight-hour day, Gaines gave his novel the feel of a Greek tragedy. While he was not conscious of alternating points of view between races, he was emphatic about balancing sections, working hard to counter the effects of tense, dramatic scenes with comic ones.

Divided into twenty chapters, the novel's action moves forward through Gaines's masterful weaving of fifteen different narrative voices encompassing an exceptionally wide range: black, white, male, female, young, old, educated, not educated, racist, liberal, and confused. All chapters are introduced by a character's name in both its formal and familiar forms (Babb, *Ernest Gaines*, 114). The formal name, for example Cyril Robillard, reflects the name on documents like birth certificates and telephone directory listings. For most of the black characters, this official name merits little recognition by the white community, reflecting their lack of access to civil rights. It's the familiar name that is known. The double identities indicate a dual consciousness. Both black and white characters are aware of the past in some form, with its lingering traditions and social customs, and the fact that these traditions are quickly fading. In some cases, the dual name may indicate continuing denigration of an individual, as is the case of Chimley. Names also reflect a social hierarchy. Thus, the "Miss" before Merle designates her as a member of the white ruling class. Community size and closeness are also reflected in name usage. That people cannot remember the formal names signals a level of physical intimacy experienced only by small groups in physically limited areas. Gaines plays upon the irony of this closeness in the final courtroom scene, when the national press laughs at the outrageousness of the men's names. As outsiders, they will never see the affection implied by their use.

Three narrative voices occur more than once: Lou Dimes, a white Baton Rouge reporter and Candy's fiance; Snookum, a black child on the plantation; and Sully, a white college student and close friend of Beau Boutan's young brother, Gil, both students at Louisiana State University (LSU). In an early version of the novel, Gaines experimented with having Lou Dimes tell the entire story but soon discovered that this narrator couldn't have access to the kind of information he would need to relate to other characters and that Lou wouldn't express himself in the kind of language Gaines wanted to include. He therefore moved into multiple first-person narratives.

All of the narrators having more than one section share an "outsider's" perspective, giving their points of view an emotional distance necessary for credibility. As a reporter, Lou remains both keenly observant and emotionally detached. His job, after all, is to record the scene before him. Aware of both the racial politics and the history of Marshall in particular and Louisiana in general, Lou instantly grasps the social dynamic before him. To Lou, the initial question isn't who *could* kill Beau but which black family *wouldn't* want to see him dead. Lou's narrative perspective also works to defuse potential shock and anger. For example, Mapes slapping Uncle Billy around has less emotional impact because Lou expects it. Lou's point of view often adds a comic perspective, as readers detect in his ironic observations of Deputy Griffin's fear when encountering armed black men.

Snookum and Sully narrate two chapters each. A child, Snookum brings to his chapters an essential innocence, honesty, and curiosity. He's bold, experimental, and adventurous, often disobeying his grandmother and every other adult present. Thanks to his disobedience, readers discover Beau Boutan's body early in the novel. They can measure the degree to which Snookum has been sheltered from history and awareness of racist terrorism in the contrast between his relating what he has seen and Janey's reaction to the news. Janey instantly panics, fearing immediate reprisals from Fix Boutan, while Snookum asks for something to eat. Snookum's role is to complicate the story by providing a generational measure between the elderly, who have been subjugated through insults and beatings, and the young, who fail to show the deference demanded by custom. Snookum's boldness is reflected in his speech when he omits to add the customary "Mr." or "Miss" when addressing white people. This anticipates a different kind of future relationship. As a child closely observing the actions of adults, Snookum absorbs the lessons of manly behavior throughout this day. He will move from fearing his younger brother's tale-telling to boldly offering himself for Sheriff Mapes to beat.

Sully also provides an outsider's point of view. Of Irish instead of French descent, he enters the narrative initially because of his friendship with Gil Boutan. A football star, Gil is the white member of a racially mixed gridiron duo, paired with Cal Harrison. Poised to become an all-American, Gil is a state hero, a media star, and a model of manhood in a state that worships football. But Sully is Cal's friend and teammate as well as Gil's. Sully is shocked when, after learning of Beau's death, Gil turns against Cal. His lack of awareness regarding the Boutan family's history with regard to race serves to increase the reliability of his observations. He can relate what he sees with an accuracy unprejudiced by family ties and a heritage of racial reprisals. One of the few college-educated characters in this novel, Sully also introduces two significant comparisons. When he first enters Marshall and sees the old men, Sully says, "It was like looking into the *Twilight Zone*" (117). And he further compares his experience to a Breughels painting. Both the television series and the paintings are suggestive of the unexpected and the surrealistic. They underscore a new dimension of reality and force a recognition of a previously unnoticed element. Sully's voice adds a metaphysical dimension which readers should not ignore.

The remaining twelve chapters are voiced by different characters, some of whom tell their own stories. While each chapter has a distinctive voice reflecting the thought processes of the character whose name introduces the chapter, many chapters allow other characters to voice their stories and some contain dramatic reportage which records what other characters say. These chapters illustrate Gaines's skill in rendering character through narrative perspective. Particularly effective are those chapters belonging to Tee Jack, the owner of the liquor and grocery store where Jack Marshall and the Klan members drink; and Sharp, a Klan member apparently less driven to violence than Luke Will. Gaines is masterful in creating the self-serving excuses of bullies and cowards. Out of their mouths flows the "justification" for brutality and racist acts that continue to echo among Klan and Nazi admirers.

But as a counterpoint to these perspectives, Gaines inserts those of characters willing to abandon the self-serving postures of Sharp and Tee Jack. These chapters have an authentic ring in voicing the self-doubt many black characters feel and in the comic badinage that lightens their moments of tension. Even Dirty Red, one of the most marginal members of the community, is given a voice and an act of personal redemption.

PLOT DEVELOPMENT

Rather than using key scenes, recurring events, or dreams to further his narrative, Gaines engages point of view as his primary device of plot development. *A Gathering of Old Men* is deliberately crowded with characters who push the sequence of action forward even as some characters reach back in time more than fifty years to recall acts justifying their presence at Mathu's house. In fact, as many as thirty-nine characters come to Mathu's house during the course of this October afternoon and evening, and most remain until the climactic action. Initially, the plot line appears linear, beginning with Candy's call to action at Aunt Glo's house and culminating in the gunfight against the Klan representatives at Mathu's. Lou Dimes's trial summary serves as an epilogue. Reading this primary plot line, readers are led to believe that the principal source of conflict lies between Mathu and Mapes, representing a racial dichotomy.

But Gaines never intended this to be a simple narrative. From the first, he complicates the action and obscures the source of conflict by having Candy deliberately withhold information from Snookum. Then he misleads readers about the motivation and identity of Beau Boutan's killer by having everyone deny the possibility of Charlie's involvement and by having Charlie remain away from the scene until the end of the novel. Because Mathu remains silent, most characters assume that he has shot Beau, and the plot seems to focus on why all these old men gather to defend Mathu. That is only a portion of a complicated plot strategy. Like many of Gaines's novels, what appears simple is a tightly woven plot. While separating all of the narrative threads would result in a lengthy discussion, isolating several may prove useful to readers.

Most of the black characters are connected to and by place, not merely St. Raphael Parish but Marshall Plantation. The graveyard scene in chapter 6 suggests more than a former physical connection to and displacement from the land. It evokes the conflicting emotions characters associate with Marshall. Out of their heritage of slavery and sharecropping, with its backbreaking labor and attendant poverty, grew a proud and tightly knit community, one now almost eradicated by the Cajuns' tractors. Many of the characters pay homage to the memory of their families, recalling both the role their families played in creating Marshall Plantation and the price they have paid for survival. More than a reminder of family history or of their own deaths, the graveyard also helps characters recall a history of injury inflicted and condoned by the white community. In fact, during this day, many characters will remember an act seeming to typify racial relations: Mat's son's needless death, Cherry Bello's sister's murder, Coot's deliberate humiliation as a returning soldier, and Silas Tucker's murder for having the energy and determination to beat Cajuns and machines. These are recalled, not simply as sources of injury but as incentive for characters to act. As Rufe observes, all had "done the same thing . . . we had all seen our brother, sister, mama, daddy insulted once and didn't do a thing about it" (97). In uniting with Mathu against what has heretofore been an unjust legal arrangement, Gaines's characters come to terms with an infinitely more complex source of conflict, an interior conflict in which one weighs survival against integrity, safety against manhood. For the elderly men, Fix and Beau represent racial oppression in the many forms all have experienced. In confronting one, the men confront all forms of racial oppression and thus redress their past deficiencies.

Gaines, however, does not make this simply a racial issue. From the beginning, he sets up Mathu and Mapes more as colleagues than adversaries, indicating a mutual respect reaching into the past. Even when the source of conflict seems to fall along color lines, he indicates a more complex interior struggle. We see this in Mathu's emotional separation from Candy throughout the text. As a white person in a prominent social position, Candy assumes that she should protect Mathu, ignoring the fact that this patronizing attitude suggests Mathu's lack of ability or authority. Mathu sees this, though, and physically separates himself from Candy, suggesting not so much disaffection with her but unity with his contemporaries who have claimed their manhood. Mathu, like many of the black characters, must struggle with his own attitudes regarding race. He tells the men that he has been proud that his Senegalese blood is untainted by "white" blood. But he comes to see that personal dignity has more to do with acts of conscience and courage than with racial purity.

Just as the black community seems divided against itself, so is the white community. We see this personified in Sheriff Mapes and Candy, who must compromise their sense of authority and accord the men at Mathu's the respect they earn and demand. Mixed attitudes toward power and race are effectively dramatized in the bar scene in chapter 13. Here, readers encounter Jack Marshall, who bears a burden of guilt over his family's slave-holding past even while he continues to support its social customs. Jack has chosen to drown his social responsibilities in alcohol rather than accept his responsibility as plantation owner and social leader. Then there is Luke Will and his group, trying to assert their power through terrorist tactics. When the professor from the University of Southwest Louisiana (USL) tries to engage Jack in some form of conversation in an attempt to have him voice a moral stand, he concludes,

"The debt is never finished as long as we stand for this [violence]" (164). Jack denies any responsibility, advising the professor to return to Texas if he cannot accept what's going on in Louisiana. This echo of regional chauvinism has a very hollow ring, as does Tee Jack's empty appeal to racial solidarity. Ultimately, of course, acts of conscience ought to be color-blind, though this has not been true in the past, when appeals to tradition and racial solidarity seemed persuasive. Now, however, as the USL professor says, "That kind of thing is over with" (157).

Gaines illustrates the obsolescence of the attitude expressed by Luke Will and his friends in Tee Jack's bar by injecting the subplot revolving around the football teamwork of Gil "Salt" Boutan and Cal "Pepper" Harrison. Here, he illustrates what everyone knows but few acknowledge: the interdependence of races and classes. This is best dramatized in the character of Gil Boutan, who represents a bridge generation between his father, Fix, and his nephew, Tee Beau. Though Gil initially claims kinship based on race with Candy, saying, "We're all made of the same bone, the same blood, the same skin" (122), he understands that family isn't sufficient. To succeed, he relies on the skill and ability of Cal. Soon after speaking to Candy, Gil says to his father, Fix, "I can't make it without Cal, Papa. I depend on him" (138). He speaks for all the characters of the community. Cal and Gil's teamwork merely reiterates that which has taken place on Marshall for over a hundred years. The difference, of course, is that Cal now gets equal credit for his accomplishments, and Gil acknowledges both Cal's skill and his right to be recognized.

This is not true of the Marshall team of Beau Boutan and Big Charlie. When we finally get to the precipitating action at the end of the novel, we learn that Beau has refused to acknowledge both the worth of Charlie's work and his status as a man. In fact, Beau is willing to kill Charlie rather than accept him as an equal, though Beau has worked closely with and profited from Charlie's labor for more than twenty years. Withholding this information until the end of the novel has two major results. First, it skillfully directs readers' attention away from the notion of a single cause and action to the *shared* issue of manhood. One by one, personal stories accumulate, illustrating a densely complex personal and racial history shared by many characters. Second, by suspending the immediate cause of Beau's death, Gaines builds the relationship of seemingly different personal experiences. Thus, when Big Charlie finally reveals how and why Beau meets his death, readers can easily see a webwork of connections to the lives and experiences of other characters. In the end, Charlie's fight is their fight, his decision to stand or die like a man is their decision.

CHARACTERIZATION

Readers might readily note that the "main" characters, seemingly Mathu and Candy, do not tell their stories. And if they are dominant figures in the novel, it is because their stories are integral to its central conflict. Orphaned at five, Candy, now thirty, has been primarily raised by Mathu and Miss Merle, a family friend, because her closest blood relatives, her Uncle Jack and Aunt Bea, are incapable of giving her any direction. Both seem to be alcoholics, more interested in liquor than in life. Shortly after Candy is left to be raised by Jack and Bea, Merle arranges a division of education. Mathu teaches Candy about "the people" while Miss Merle schools her in southern ladyhood. As we can see from Candy's passionate attachment to Mathu and her patronizing sense of loyalty, both have been successful in imparting lessons. Trying to be true to her heritage, Candy takes charge, feeling responsible for the safety of "her people." Certain of Mathu's guilt, Candy orchestrates the gathering, anticipates Sheriff Mapes, and then steps forward to assume responsibility once Mapes arrives. Her color, gender, and social position provide all the protective armor she needs. Candy Marshall is clearly a character to reckon with, and she's also one to observe closely. Her physical proximity to Mathu throughout the novel attests to her deep concern for him. It also suggests her emotional dependence. Much of their relationship, however, is not expressed through words. Here, merely a word or a gesture suggests volumes. Believing that only she can protect the black residents of Marshall against Mapes and the Boutans, Candy fails to listen to anyone else. Only late in the story, when Mathu speaks to her, does she begin to listen.

Their physical separation, indicating an emotional break, comes at the insistence of the old men, and it forces her to reluctantly recognize an already changed relationship. To Candy, Mathu embodies the soul of Marshall, with its history of work and sacrifice. To lose Mathu means losing Marshall, as Candy indicates when she says, "They [her father and grandfather] said if you went, it went, because we could not—it could not—not without you, Mathu" (177). In accepting her role as responsible owner, Candy has failed to grasp the fundamental inequality of their relationship that offers protection for submission. On this day, Candy will be forced to see Mathu as an individual capable of fighting his own battles.

Of course, one of the many ironies of this novel is that Mathu has been defending his honor throughout his life. All of the characters pay respect to him because of his absolute refusal to diminish himself for anyone. The story of Mathu's fight with Fix Boutan rather than return Fix's pop bottle has become community legend. One of the oldest living residents on Marshall, Mathu is proud of his pure Senegalese heritage, but he comes to characterize himself not as a hero but "a mean, bitter old man" who has placed "myself above all" (182). Characterizing his pride as a form of hatred, he has lived life hating whites for their refusal to acknowledge his citizenship and other blacks for their reluctance to become citizens. Mathu's anger, as Daniel White has observed, has kept him from balancing his commanding influence with understanding (White, "Haunted by the Idea," 173). But during this day, along with the other old men, Mathu changes. Perhaps he even changes the most, attributing his pride not to his acts but to those of the men around him.

Rather than individualize a single character to represent a group of people and/or idea, Gaines creates a group as his "principal" character. He wanted the *men* to be important, not simply a single character. Still, he individualizes his characters not only by color and nickname but through language and gesture. Dirty Red always seems to have a soggy, ash-laden, self-rolled cigarette hanging from his lip. Mapes rolls a Lifesaver around his mouth. Deputy Griffin pulls his gun when he feels safe and abandons it when he feels threatened. All of these gestures indicate something essential about their natures. Gaines heightens reader awareness of character differences through their nicknames: Coot, Rooster, Cherry Red, Rufe, Clabber, and Chimley. Some names, like Clabber, Cherry, and Chimley, suggest skin color, while others, like Rooster, suggest stature and temperament. Nicknames also draw readers into immediate intimacy, bypassing formalities. Just as he does in other novels, Gaines distinguishes each character through grammar, repetition, dialect, sentence structure, and tone. Janey's panicked pleas to Jesus suggest more than fear; they indicate her religious faith and her sense of powerlessness. Lou Dimes's ironic reportage in standard English indicates an emotional distance in addition to education and profession. *A Gathering of Old Men* is literally a *tour de force* of characterization through language, indicating Gaines's genius in creating individual characters with remarkable economy.

THEMATIC CONCERNS AND LITERARY DEVICES

As the novel's title suggests, *A Gathering of Old Men* has as its thematic center the subject of manhood. This is a recurring issue in Gaines's fiction because of its personal and general resonance. Gaines's story deliberately concentrates on men, with little space given to female characters or experiences. When women are a part of the narrative, it's often to heighten a weak male self-image because one of the characteristics of manhood seems to be the privilege of ordering women around. Thus, Chimley derives some pleasure from commanding his wife to have his fish cleaned when he returns, and Lou Dimes gets ridiculed because Candy won't obey him. But this definition of manhood—and many others— will prove false during the day.

Throughout the novel, various examples of "manhood" are offered. Despite their attempts to live up to these examples, most male characters have been denied status as men, primarily because of race. Many of the men relate personal tales suggesting their sense of failure. Most stories revolve around an inability to protect family members. Mat, Cherry, Billy, and Gable, for example, recognize their ineffectiveness against a social and economic system that denies them access and ignores their existence. Someone they love is denied hospital care, legal access, or humane treatment by social institutions charged with particular responsibilities. Coot, who believes he has earned status as a man through his military service, is threatened with injury if he's seen wearing his World War I uniform. The standard of manhood has, for the most part, depended upon the subjugation of someone or something. And it has personal risk as its price. All of the black characters recall insults, threats, beatings—some form of humiliation carried out to diminish their sense of Self. But during this day, each character learns that being a man does not depend upon diminishing the worth of others. It does, however, mean demanding recognition of one's worth—even when defense of personal dignity leads to violence. Most of all, manhood includes taking responsibility for one's actions and a willingness to face the consequences of those actions. As Charlie says late in the novel, "A nigger boy run and run and run. But a man come back" (187).

What Charlie learns in the swamp is similar to the lesson the old men absorb in the graveyard. Here, the spirits of the past seem to speak to the men, reminding them of their mortality and the dignity of human endeavor. There's more nourishment than that provided by the pecans, though the rich nuts signify the presence of life. In the graveyard, the men put aside their differences of color and status and engage in each other's lives. Recognizing the possible price of their acts, they rise above personal concerns, committing both to each other and to the task at hand. Clatoo, who assumes leadership, gives everyone an opportunity to turn away, and when no one does, he shows his pride and confidence in the men by announcing that they are going in like soldiers, not tramps. Late in the novel, readers learn that the land has communicated a similar message to Charlie, who cannot leave Marshall because an invisible wall prevents his escape. Once Charlie stops to listen, he hears "a voice calling me back here" (193). Having sparked Beau's brutality by insisting that Beau respect his age, if nothing else, Charlie comes to understand that he must fight his own battle instead of hiding behind his godfather, Mathu. Moreover, Charlie refuses to back away from the threatened actions of Luke Will, whose sense of worth, like Beau's, depends upon Charlie's fear and self-abasement. In fact, Charlie will take the lead in directing the shooting, as Luke Will acknowledges when he tells Sharp that Mapes isn't in charge: "Charlie is. We got to deal with Charlie now" (206).

While the issue of manhood is one all of the old men come to terms with, Gaines makes sure readers understand that manhood is *everyone's* issue, everyone's fight. The reason why this is so important is that it moves to the core of social injustice. Gaines's novel illustrates an overwhelmingly patriarchal social order, one dependent upon a diminished class of people deprived of both political and economic power, denied legal protection, and subject to culturally sanctioned acts of violence— at least this has been true in the past. As long as the men collude in their own abasement, they perpetuate a system, even though it has become completely ineffectual. Readers see this most clearly in the characters of Jack Marshall and Fix Boutan. Jack will have no part of any business, passing responsibility to Candy, who, as a woman, lacks authority in any patriarchal system. Try as she might to affect being male, with her khaki slacks and short hair, Candy wields less authority than Jack, though Jack is utterly passive. Fix also finds his strength diminished by time and change. Gil's shame over his family's reputation for brutal racist acts prevents Fix from supporting more violence, not because he believes his impulse wrong but because two sons express the obsolescence of his ideas. Fix believes that retribution against the black community defends his family honor and thus insists upon family unity before he acts. Without complete accord, Fix has no motive other than personal revenge, and he refuses to go against the decision of the male members of his family, despite his voiced contempt for their objections. Gil and Jean, motivated in part by personal costs, force their father to recognize that times have changed.

In fact, change is another theme of this novel, a theme expressed through image and action. Once again Gaines's fiction dramatizes the economic impact mechanization has on the black community. He places Beau's running tractor in a prominent position and calls attention to its impact throughout the novel. For twenty-five years the Boutans have leased Marshall land, using tractors instead of people to work the cane fields. Given the most productive land to farm because of skin color, the Boutans have increased their productivity and economic security while the Marshall residents have lost theirs. Tractors, then, threaten the survival of the Marshall community, now populated by old people and children as young adults have left the land for jobs elsewhere. Moreover, tractors threaten the very memory of what Marshall residents have contributed.

When the old folks of Marshall look around, they see weeds, suggestive of untended land. Early in the novel, John Paul asks people what they don't see. Then he recalls a vital community of the past, bound by work, stories, song, prayer, and four-o'clocks. A community that tended the land, drawing life from it and giving life back to the land. Now people see rotting houses and weed-covered plots. Even the graveyard seems threatened, and with it the memory of what Marshall residents have made. Thus, John Paul claims that he's standing up for his "own people" and "for every four-o'clock, every rosebush, every palm-of-Christian ever growed on this place" (92).

A Gathering of Old Men deals with another, less visible change as well, a change in social and legal status. In short, the novel deals with changing racial relations. Everyone at Marshall assumes that Fix Boutan, with friends and relatives, will exact a violent revenge for Beau's death. This includes Sheriff Mapes, who hopes to avert violence by making a quick arrest. Mapes's initially brutal tactics suggest that little has changed regarding the legal status of black residents. Indeed, most characters, having been victims of an unjust system, assume that Mapes's presence is to victimize, not protect. But Mapes changes during this long afternoon and evening, his respect growing as he hears their stories. Thus, in the end, he can call Charlie "Mr. Biggs" with genuine respect.

Mapes also points out a changed social status to black residents. When they learn that Fix is not coming, they feel deprived of an opportunity to assert their worth. Sheriff Mapes calls attention to an essential contradiction in their response, saying, "You told God you wanted Salt and Pepper to get together, and God did it for you. At the same time, you wanted God to keep Fix the way Fix was thirty years ago, so one day you would get a chance to shoot him. Well, God couldn't do both" (171). This social change has been signaled first by Mapes's efforts to protect the people at Marshall, and it is later reiterated in the courtroom when Judge Reynolds sentences black and white defendents equally. These actions signal a dramatic shift in the legal status of black characters who are finally recognized as citizens.

Readers should pay careful attention to Gaines's use of three major images throughout the novel: guns, tractors, weeds, and cultivated plants. Candy's initial order is for men to come with twelve-gauge shotguns and empty number-five shells. She insists that the men shoot before arriving. This makes sense from her perspective, since Candy hopes to frustrate the immediate arrest of Mathu by confusing both the sheriff and the forensic evidence. But the empty shotgun suggests a certain impotence as well. The men appear armed but really have no power to defend themselves or others while their guns are unloaded. Clatoo, however, has brought extra shells, and he orchestrates a means by which the men discreetly reload their guns without drawing the notice of Candy and Sheriff Mapes. Thus, Candy and Mapes see old men with unloaded guns and assume their ineffectiveness. When the men reveal that they have loaded their shotguns, they announce their readiness to defend their manhood. In the end, the men direct the action, literally calling the shots, while Candy and Mapes do nothing.

The tractor, as suggested earlier, emblematizes agricultural mechanization, a changed relationship not merely between people and the land but people and people. It condemns past practices, distances people from land, and threatens the past. Sitting atop a diesel tractor, Fix and Beau Boutan have a fundamentally different relationship with the land than they would working it by hand and mule. They cannot smell, see, or feel the immediate textures of fieldwork. Fix's attention is on completing the maximum labor with the fewest workers. Workers, like machines, exist to labor tirelessly and merit neither respect nor praise. When they wear out, they are replaced. The tractor doesn't merely displace people, though a major consequence of its use is to drive young adults on Marshall away from a way of life to find another livelihood. The tractor also changes the relationship between two competing groups, people who actually have much in common. Given the advantage of the best land to farm, Fix, with his tractor, can believe himself a superior farmer. His machine increases his productivity—and his ambition. He wants to lease the entire Marshall Plantation, though the result is to drive off the people who have lived there and worked the land for five generations. Tucker's story of his brother, Silas, the last black sharecropper at Marshall, illustrates the role of the tractor in distancing people from each other. Driving himself and his mules to exhaustion, Silas manages to beat Fix to the cane derrick. Because a human being isn't supposed to win against machines, and no black man can appear superior to a white man, Silas is murdered, beaten to death by Cajuns. Technology, then, alters values. By changing the means of competition, Fix also alters the ends. Farming becomes a business instead of a life. Since the end of business is profit, nothing else matters—not the people and certainly not the past.

The past is largely recalled through cultivated plants, especially four-o'clocks. These late-afternoon bloomers, with their sugary lemon scent, characterize a time before tractors, a Quarters free of weeds, and a way of life when people related to each other as well as to plant and animal life. In recalling the four-o'clocks, Johnny Paul doesn't sentimentalize the past. He respects the difficulty of the labor, but he also recognizes the value of a community bound by mutual care and respect. Their absence is measured in weeds, which indicate a lack of attention to the land.

A MARXIST READING

Most of Gaines's fiction readily lends itself to a Marxist interpretation, but his novels set on a single plantation seem especially focused on a conflict between those who control the land, politics, and society and those who submit to this control. For a more complete definition of Marxist theory, one might review the critical interpretation section of *Of Love and Dust*. But a brief summary of some basic Marxist views should be helpful here. Marx claims that: (1) more than any other factor, economics—defined as our changing means of material production—determines human history, creating our social relations, institutions, and ideology; (2) changes in the means of production create changes in social class structures resulting in a struggle for political, social, and economic advantage; and (3) human beliefs—our ways of thinking, feeling, and explaining—reflect the particular interests of a specific class and work to both legitimize and perpetuate the interests of the dominant economic and social class. Marxist critics will generally focus on the author's worldview, the time in which the text is written, and the time of the fiction, giving particular attention to sources of conflict. In short, a Marxist critic will examine a text, largely concentrating on its presentation of economic and social forces rather than paying attention to such aesthetic devices as imagery, paradox, or symbolism. Given the prominence of the tractor signifying a changed means of production in *A Gathering of Old Men*, a Marxist interpretation seems appropriate.

Ernest Gaines most frequently sets his fiction in the 1930s and 1940s, not only because he lived in south Louisiana during that time and was strongly influenced by the people around him but also because that period is so thematically rich. Gaines's worldview offers readers a bridge between an essentially nineteenth-century way of life, with mules and men doing most of the labor, and a twentieth-century way of life, with its machines. His fiction focuses on the structure of society, a stratified system favoring some people over others on the basis of birth and gender, and it often reflects the changes that have resulted from technology. Most importantly, from a Marxist critic's perspective, is that Gaines's fiction encourages readers to discover the relationships among history, technology, social and political movements, and art. While a close reading of Gaines's work will result in an understanding of its organic unity, a Marxist reading will draw attention to its historic and social dimensions.

Written twenty years after the peak of civil rights activities in the South, *A Gathering of Old Men* reflects changing social relationships. Mechanization has altered a lingering way of life—a way of life that persists in people's memories and in social custom. Tractors have displaced an entire class of people, forcing them away from the plantation to make a new livelihood. Tractors have also changed the social structure, for as the Cajuns gain economic power, they claim an enhanced social status rather than accept their previous classification as field labor. A Marxist critic might look closely at the value system of the Boutan family, noting how it emulates the values of the Marshalls, with its essentially exploitative basis. Gil's claim of kinship to Candy would have particular resonance, then, because they are alike in their belief of social dominance based on skin color. Though they express sympathy for the conditions of black characters, Gil and Candy have nevertheless operated on an assumption of privilege.

Certainly, a Marxist critic would concentrate on the values of the Marshalls, exposing their corruption. These decadent values, indicated through Jack and Bea's childlessness, their inability to raise Candy, and their daily cycle of drinking and napping, are defunct. Nothing on Marshall Plantation claims their labor or care. Jack and Bea take responsibility neither for the raising of their own nor for the nurturance of others who depend upon them. Though the Marshalls seem to remain above conflict, they have really created it and support its continuance because it favors their dominance. As long as the central conflict seems to be between Cajuns and blacks, Jack and Bea Marshall can appear isolated and superior. Alcoholic and incompetent, they enjoy their position at the top of a social hierarchy, a position that accords them respect and service from others without their having to show any regard for other people. Jack Marshall's character would merit more attention than Bea's; as the last male Marshall descendent, he represents economic and social traditions based on the complete exploitation of human labor through slavery. Jack clearly is obsolete, his language revealing an inability to see blacks as human. To him, the people at Marshall "belong" to Candy (159), like any possession.

Candy Marshall would be exposed for sharing these values. One of the major conflicts in this novel is dramatized through Candy and Mathu. In one sense, Mathu is Candy's father, literally raising her in a tradition separate from the one Miss Merle teaches. Mathu's job is to teach Candy about the people on Marshall, but his admission to the men about his own scorn for them underscores his sense of elitism and separation similar to that of the Marshalls. Candy does have a sense of responsibility to everyone remaining on the plantation, especially Mathu. But, as the novel reveals, her "love" is conditional. When the men announce that Candy cannot be a part of their discussion, she threatens to evict them, a gesture indicative of her belief in the old system. Mathu will change his allegiance from Candy to the men, suggesting his discovery of and faith in their newly claimed individual power, but Candy will remain the same. In the end, she seems not to understand exactly what has happened, and she reaches for Lou's hand in a gesture of need. What Candy fails to acknowledge are such historical factors as the Civil Rights movement.

The Civil Rights movement worked to eliminate laws specifically passed to limit the social interaction, education, and political access of black citizens. In other words, the movement worked to make Americans of African descent full citizens. Long denied a role in American politics, black citizens found a voice first in leaders like Dr. Martin Luther King, Jr., then on a more personal basis, and began using their newly claimed political power. *A Gathering of Old Men* dramatizes the empowerment of a small group. Part of the narrative's momentum depends upon internal conflicts as various characters weigh personal safety against a claim of manhood. Gaines employs the metaphors of crawling under the bed versus marching in like soldiers to indicate a progression of physical (and psychological) stature for his characters. This gradual claim to place and voice is guided first by Clatoo, but it later assumes a momentum of its own. When Luke Will and his buddies announce their presence, all of the men step forward to fight, no longer needing a leader. Fanning out over the Quarters and taking turns hooting and shooting, they act independently instead of at someone's command. In the end, the novel suggests a redistribution of power—or at least an initial recognition of its redistribution, one more equitable in its application of justice.

One question a Marxist critic will ask revolves around the social controls at work within each group. And that brings us to an analysis of Luke Will's role in this novel. Luke Will is Fix Boutan's apparent successor as an extralegal social control. Both seem to operate without fear of arrest or even social sanction, suggesting not merely the support but the approval of those in positions of social and political authority. Fix, however, limits his violence, using family as his rationale. Without family unanimity, he won't terrorize the old people and children of Marshall. In contrast, Luke Will and his buddies have neither internal nor external controls, nothing, at any rate, that cannot be overcome by alcohol. Driven by blind hatred to support his feeble sense of manhood, Luke Will's only claim to power derives from terrorizing others, and the legal apparatus proves ineffectual in controling his actions. Thus, a wounded Mapes significantly sits in front of Mathu's steps, unable to rise during the shooting. Luke Will becomes a logical extension of Jack Marshall. Underscoring the hollowness of Marshall's social position, Luke Will represents an extremely decadent social system, absent of any moral responsibility.

Gaines's focus on various social levels—and especially his characterization of the disenfranchised, his depiction of those who control the means of production, his portrayal of those who threaten the *status quo*, and his emphasis on a changing social system—mark him as an author whose fiction presents an alternative view. It invites readers to participate in various levels of a class struggle as it relates the seemingly unrelated. Fusing form to message, Gaines creates in *A Gathering of Old Men* a revolutionary novel, a perceptive social critique, and an exacting portrayal of gradual human improvement.

8

A Lesson Before Dying
(1994)

The year 1993 was an exceptionally good one for Ernest Gaines. Turning sixty, he married for the first time, won the MacArthur award, and published *A Lesson Before Dying*. Gaines had invested seven years in the writing of this novel, a book which echoes with familiar themes and characters. Set in Bayonne in 1948, *A Lesson Before Dying* centers around the education of two men: Grant Wiggins, a college-trained teacher in his early thirties; and Jefferson, a twenty-one-year-old field-worker condemned to death for a crime he did not commit. During his trial, Jefferson's defense attorney will argue that electrocuting his client would be like executing a hog; thus stripping his client of his very humanity and rudimentary self-esteem. Recruited by his Aunt Lou and Jefferson's godmother, Miss Emma, to teach Jefferson how to die like a man, Grant will, in the process, learn much about how to live. The lessons both men absorb concern the meaning of manhood.

Gaines had originally set his novel in 1988. However, unable to receive an answer from the warden of Angola Prison regarding whether a teacher could visit a death-row prisoner, he turned back in time to write a different novel, set in a period when racism was open and casual. Supplementing his own experience and knowledge by talking with sheriffs and death-row lawyers, Gaines blended factual details, such as Louisiana's portable electric chair and the day and time of all state

executions, with a created but representative experience regarding responsibility, justice, and human dignity.

STRUCTURE AND POINT OF VIEW

The novel's action opens in late October, during the sugarcane harvest,
and concludes soon after Easter in April, with the beginning of planting
season. This six-month period comprises the academic year for Grant,
when he teaches the children from the Pichot Plantation in his one-room
school along with Jefferson. Six months also suggest the half measures
of institutionalized education and justice accorded African Americans.
While all of the physical supports of equal treatment, such as books and
defense lawyers, seem to be in place, they are merely a sham. We see
this immediately in Grant's account of Jefferson's trial. Though Grant
has not been present, knowing in advance what the outcome will be, he
feels as if he had been there precisely because the proceedings are so
predictable. Furnished with the apparatus of American "justice," Jefferson's trial looks like any other, with his court-appointed defense attorney, prosecutor, jury, and judge—all white and all male. And the
conduct of the trial contains some revealing practices, especially on the
part of Jefferson's lawyer. First of all, he doesn't ask Jefferson to tell his
story, thus denying him voice. Instead, his lawyer tells Jefferson's story
and in the process characterizes his client as "it," "this," "thing," and
"fool" (7). He continues his appeal to the jury's prejudices by referring
to the shape of Jefferson's head as well as other physical and racial characteristics that seem to separate Jefferson from them. In fact, his oblique
reference to the nineteenth-century "science" of phrenology, which
"measured" character and intellectual capacity by the shape of the skull,
emphasizes that there has been no change of mind regarding the legal
and intellectual status of blacks since the nineteenth-century, when
blacks were legally defined as property, not as human beings (Babb,
"Old Fashioned Modernism," 253). His ultimate argument, however,
that justice would not be served by killing Jefferson since executing him
would be like executing "a hog" not only denies the essential humanity
of his client, it equates Jefferson with a domestic animal that generally
thrives on scraps, lives in squalor, and is associated with utter unclean-
liness. The courtroom scene, then, dramatizes and contains the ugly truth
of how denial of legal rights and intellectual training have worked to
imprison African Americans from their earliest days in this country.

The six months of Jefferson's imprisonment parallel the academic year for Grant's students, a "year" fully three months shorter than that of white students. Gaines plays on the legal justification of "separate but equal," exposing its inequities in one of the novel's strongest scenes, when the school superintendent arrives for his annual visit. Grant will point out that Dr. Joseph Morgan visits the black schools only once each year while visiting the white schools twice. Throughout the visit, Grant will address the superintendent as "Dr. Joseph," his address suggestive of both familiarity and deference as he places the title with Morgan's first name. In contrast, Dr. Morgan's lack of interest in Grant or his mission is indicated by his repeated and mistaken address of Grant as "Higgins" instead of "Wiggins," even after Grant introduces himself. More significant, though, is what Morgan chooses to inspect: hands, teeth, bible verses, and pledge of allegiance. These are telling indicators of what those in authority consider valuable as the children's education. Recognizing Morgan's inspection of the children's teeth as being similar to that of a slave buyer, Grant ironically notes that "At least Dr. Joseph had graduated to the level where he let the children spread their own lips" (56). Declaring Grant's students a "good crop," and leaving them with a lecture on nutrition and the virtue of hard work, Morgan shows little interest in their intellectual achievements, and he dismisses Grant's indirect plea for more school supplies and textbooks without missing pages. His final words urging more flag drill ring with irony since the final phrase of the pledge promises "liberty and justice for all." Morgan's visit reaffirms Grant's belief that no matter what he teaches, his students will continue to be field-workers, and it sharpens Grant's growing awareness of the connection between his students and Jefferson.

A Lesson Before Dying breaks into three distinctive parts told from differing perspectives. Chapters 1–28 and the concluding chapter 31, are told from Grant Wiggin's point of view. Chapter 29 is Jefferson's prison diary during the last weeks of his life. And chapter 30 is told from several narrative perspectives by members of the community as they feel the impact of Jefferson's execution. These strategic shifts work to create a more comprehensive view than a single narrative angle, they detail Grant's frustration as he struggles with emotional demands he would rather avoid, and they avoid stereotypical community responses on execution day. Most important, perhaps, is the role Jefferson's diary plays. Throughout most of the novel Jefferson is silent, his lack of voice indicative of both his rage and inability to be heard. Convinced that no one will accord him human dignity, Jefferson avoids language because "hogs don't talk." Encouraged by Grant to write down anything that comes to him, Jefferson begins to reclaim his voice and stature.

Grant's narrative perspective is significant for a number of reasons. As a member of a small, intimate community, he has direct knowledge of gesture and nuance—the unspoken rules of behavior and expectation. Thus, he can literally feel his Aunt Lou's eyes on various parts of his body and correctly interpret their meaning as well as give readers the actual meaning of such apparently simple words as "here." Having grown up on the Pichot Plantation, Grant is aware of community history and the unspoken rules of caste and class. He can correctly and eloquently interpret the many silences so important to understanding, telling readers, for example, how Pichot's gardener, Farell Jarreau, must gather information "by stealth or through an innate sense of things around him" (41). At the same time, Grant is also one of the few college-educated characters in the novel, and this makes him an anomaly not only because his grammar marks him as different from most characters—white or black—but because his experience has been broadened outside this confining system. Thus, Grant feels like an outsider, existing on the margins of his society, even while he is an insider. His feeling of estrangement and his reluctance to be involved add to his reliability as a narrator because readers understand that he acts and reports more out of honest duty than from personal interest.

Grant's position is similar to that of Jim Kelly in *Of Love and Dust*. Both men become reluctant instructors for difficult characters, and, like Jim, Grant will change. Grant's uniquely marginal status is important because it allows him to see quite clearly what goes on and to relate it in standard English. At the same time, Grant must have intimate knowledge so he can correctly interpret the meaningful silences and atmospheric nuances that comprise an essential part of human communication, especially among the oppressed. Thus, acting as a sort of translator, Grant becomes a conduit effecting communal change. His emotional distance is both an essential component of his character and his narrative reliability. Feeling superior to Jefferson, Grant believes that he has nothing to gain through their relationship. But he will, like Jim Kelly, reverse his initial opinion of his doomed student, coming to admire him. This transformation will carry in its wake Grant's changing attitudes toward the children he teaches, his religious belief, and his need for emotional commitment. At the novel's end, Grant, the most detached and eloquent character, will be unable to express the depth of his feelings in words.

By contrast, Jefferson's diary, coming from the opposite direction, reveals a character whose humanity grows through the process of writing. Gaines's decision to give Jefferson a written method of expression does more than allow him his silence throughout the novel, a silence that tells readers the depth of his lawyer's insult and the degree of Jefferson's rage. His diary, with its lack of capitalization and punctuation and its phonetic spelling, begins with the statement that he has nothing to say, thus suggesting Jefferson's lack of voice and purpose. With Grant's encouragement, however, subsequent passages quickly summarize his representative history, including Boo's rebellious example and Jefferson's admiration of him. Thus, readers are given a glimpse of spirit they couldn't otherwise detect.

Like many students, Jefferson asks for a grade on his assignment, wanting Grant to place a value on his written expression of his emerging Self (Babb, "Old Fashioned Modernism," 252). This accounts for Jefferson's expression of disappointment when Grant, wanting him to plunge deeper into his consciousness, gives him a "B" instead of an "A." Once Jefferson begins to write about the difficult subject of love, Grant raises his grade to an encouraging "B+." At this point, the diary conveys more strength and insight revealed by Jefferson's claim that he knows the true characters of those around him, even though he has never said so. Jefferson's spelling of "human" as "youman" emphasizes his kinship to all members of the community, including his jailers. And his value and relationship to the community are later underscored by their visits. As this chapter progresses, readers can trace Jefferson's growing concern for others' feelings when he writes that he has let Emma hold him for as long as she needs to, when he apologizes to Grant for having insulted Vivian, and most of all when he patiently waits for Bok, a mentally retarded character, to find an appropriate marble as a farewell gift. As Jefferson reclaims his humanity through language, his diary gains eloquence so that the last few lines command the power of poetry.

Chapter 30, written mainly from the third-person omniscient point of view, recounts execution day through the varying impressions and actions of the Bayonne community. From Sidney deRogers's inattentiveness when the truck transporting the electric chair rumbles into town to the callous comments of a white sales clerk, readers are asked to witness a cross section of responses. By this means, Gaines maintains control over an emotionally charged situation. The fiction sustains its integrity without its author having to resort to such artificial and didactic methods as farewell speeches or melodramatic action. The very ordinariness of this chapter is the thematic point, which is further emphasized by its significant organization. Essentially, chapter 30 is a community catalog organized around the arrival and installation of the state's portable electric chair. After introducing the truck's image, successive sections will flash back to the night before, with the sleeplessness of those characters most affected by Jefferson's death: Aunt Lou, Miss Emma, Vivian, Grant, and Reverend Ambrose. Then the chapter takes readers through the morning preparations: from Sheriff Guidry's avoiding eye contact with his wife at breakfast, to the truck's appearance and courthouse worker's interest in the chair's installation, to the generator hum as Bayonne literally vibrates with its current, and, finally to the physical preparation of Jefferson for execution. Embedding a good deal of authentic information in deceptively simple prose, Gaines's verbal restraint triggers unexpected emotions, his objective invisibility the measure of an exceptional writer.

PLOT DEVELOPMENT

As suggested by the novel's title, *A Lesson Before Dying* is structured largely through dramatic incidents in which the two main characters teach and learn from each other how to be men. This is a particularly difficult lesson because there are few models, little encouragement, and three hundred years of history working against them. Reviewing the lessons of living and dying around them, however, Grant and Jefferson will teach each other much about the essentials of true character.

When the novel opens, readers will experience, along with Grant and Jefferson, primarily lessons that deny manhood status to all males of African heritage. The legal classification of black Americans as "chattel," or movable property, is a matter of historic record. From their earliest days in this country, black men have been thought of and called something other than men. These continuing denials, based on race, are explicit in forms of address like "boy." Bayonne, Louisiana, in 1948 shows little indication of having changed its racial attitudes from those of a century ago. Thus, readers witness casual, everyday occurrences of personal insult designed to keep black people humble and intimidated, in other words, "in their place." Since Grant has either been spared or has avoided much contact with the white power structure after his return to Bayonne, he must undergo a form of reindoctrination. He therefore enters through the back door to the Pichot Plantation, waits in the kitchen two and a half hours while the white folks eat their dinner, submits to other deliberate delays and searches at the jail, and holds his temper while being interrogated about his plans. These customary practices, designed to indicate Grant's reduced social importance, also bring home the lesson that he and Jefferson share more commonalities than differences.

Grant's education takes place in unlikely classrooms: the Rainbow Club and his room in Aunt Lou's house. Listening to two men in the Rainbow Club discuss Jackie Robinson's baseball feats, Grant connects this popular athletic hero to literary art by associating Robinson with Joe Louis and both with the James Joyce story, "Ivy Day in the Committee Room." His apparently free association demonstrates to him how, rising from ordinary circumstances, the hero inspires pride in others. In other words, he is made to think about the role a hero can play in the community. Grant's lesson centers, then, on individual actions that defy public expectation.

Grant also receives instruction from the women in his life, especially Aunt Lou and Vivian. Aunt Lou, of course, is memorable as a character who affects Grant by merely looking at him, her expectations of appropriate behavior long since implanted in him. Although Grant will at one point accuse Aunt Lou of helping white people instruct him in humiliation, he is usually conscious of her moral example and silent expectation. Grant uses the word "boulder" to describe both Lou and Emma, a word evoking their strength, endurance, and immovability. Aunt Lou obviously volunteers Grant's services to teach Jefferson, insists upon his appearance at the Pichot Plantation, and expects his visits and consideration of both Miss Emma and Jefferson—all without her saying so. Refusing to hear Grant's reasons for giving up, Aunt Lou exerts a moral pull. Late in the novel, Grant will tell Vivian that Aunt Lou requires from him exactly what Emma wants from Jefferson: a memory to be proud of after three hundred years of "failure" (166–67). If Aunt Lou holds Grant to a standard from the past, Vivian Babtiste presents an even stronger link to the future. Gaines has said that her role in the novel is to keep Grant in the community. Still married to another man and the mother of two small children, Vivian, a Roman Catholic, faces a number of restraints binding her to Bayonne. Vivian has already proven her willingness to make personal sacrifices for her beliefs through her commitment to teaching and to Grant. A light-skinned Creole rejected by her own family because she associates with darker-skinned people, she rejects discrimination based on color. She becomes Grant's anchor, providing both encouragement and support when he most needs it and rejecting his pleas that they simply run away.

But it is Reverend Ambrose who possibly imparts the most important lesson by providing the missing block in Grant's education. This scene, occurring at the end of chapter 27, brings the apparent conflict between religion and reason to a climax. Like many of Gaines's protagonists, Grant has turned away from the church, finding its dependence on simple faith an inadequate justification for and management of the multiple injustices encountered by African Americans. Lacking belief in the power of the church, Grant feels suspended between two worlds, the past and the future. Despite Reverend Ambrose's urging, Grant has consistently resisted encouraging Jefferson to find comfort in prayer because he believes he owes Jefferson the truth. But Grant's thinly concealed contempt for Ambrose is replaced by a dawning understanding of his self-sacrifice for the good of the whole when Ambrose explains what Grant doesn't see. Saying that he lies to "relieve hurt" hidden from the eyes of others, Ambrose directs Grant's attention to Aunt Lou: "You ever looked at the scabs on her knees, boy? Course you never. 'Cause she never wanted you to see it" (218). And the reason, Ambrose concludes, that people cheat themselves and lie to those they love is their hope "that one they all love and trust can come back and help relieve the pain" (218).

Relieving Jefferson's pain will prove to be acutely difficult not only because of the physical and temporal limitations set by authorities but also because Jefferson proves an exceptionally unresponsive student. Hurt and self-absorbed, he initially tries to live *down* to his lawyer's description of him as a hog. Refusing to eat or respond to his visitors, he thus causes more anguish for his godmother, Emma. When Grant tries to make him see how his responses affect others, Jefferson retaliates by striking out at Grant. He insults Vivian and then threatens to scream, an act that will put an end to Grant's visits. Sensing for the first time Jefferson's need, Grant calls his bluff, telling him to scream if he wants to. Though Jefferson again tries to provoke Grant by continuing to insult Vivian, Grant now perceives what he had started to suspect, the pain beneath the grin. On his next visit, Grant will define the meaning of "moral" and "obligation," thus beginning the intellectual aspect of his instruction.

Before he is ready for this level of instruction, Jefferson must come to know that he has a place in his community. Grant ensures this through having the children of his school work to purchase a Christmas gift for Jefferson, by imparting community news to him, and by buying him a radio. This last gift—obtained through cash gifts from several Bayonne citizens, including Grant—links Jefferson to the outside world even as he uses it to drown out interior thoughts. Significantly, it is one of the few new items ever purchased for Jefferson, and he keeps it on constantly, showing both a childlike obsession with it as well as his need for company. Having established Jefferson's humanity and his connection to others, Grant moves into a more challenging phase of instruction. After "moral" and "obligation," he defines "hero" as one who "does something that other men don't and can't do" (191). A hero, Grant continues, is something that he cannot be. Only Jefferson has the potential to rise beyond expectation to expose the "old lie" of myth for what it is (192). That Jefferson has absorbed the lessons Grant teaches becomes evident in his changing behavior.

CHARACTERIZATION

Gaines creates his main character, Grant Wiggins, largely through explicit presentation. In other words, we see who Grant is through what he says and does. Early in the novel, Grant will ask three perennial human questions: "Who am I?" "Do I know what a man is?" and "What will I have accomplished?" (31). That Grant asks these questions in relation to Jefferson doesn't lessen their personal impact because, having been asked to teach Jefferson his value as a man, Grant must inevitably discover his own. While Grant would like to believe that he's emotionally and physically isolated from Jefferson, he must discover their mutual human characteristics. To do this, he must own up to his deficiencies. Initially, readers encounter a character who says that he is detached and yet demonstrates barely controlled anger. The sources of Grant's anger are everywhere since he is an educated black man living in the deep South after World War II. While there are abundant signs of technological change, social and legal changes have not yet occurred. Thus, Grant is allowed only one profession, and even this is limited by a white power structure. Not only does Grant actively hate teaching, he believes that his efforts are wasted since his students will have little choice other than to become field-workers. Living in a region that denies him manhood and working at a job he believes to be futile, Grant dreams of a life where he might enjoy choice. When Aunt Lou insists that Grant assume the seemingly impossible task of teaching Jefferson how to be a man, Grant is understandably angry since this, too, will add to his sense of failure.

What, then, changes him? First, he must review the lessons of his own life. Grant recalls his teacher at Pichot, Matthew Antoine, a Creole who openly hated his students because they were darker than he and who taught them only one lesson: leave the South. Filled with self-hatred, Antoine's parting advice to Grant—"forget about life"—denies any value of living (65). A young man, Grant is understandably reluctant to accept this negative instruction, recognizing that Antoine merely reiterates the white rationale for denying human value to blacks. When Aunt Lou insists that Grant endure routine humiliations—which she has worked to spare him for ten years—she assists in his review of social practices designed to indicate the reduced value of blacks. Thus, when Grant enters the Pichot house using the back door, waits in the kitchen, and submits to searches at the jail, he undergoes a form of reindoctrination to the multiple social gestures denying his human value. Every time he meets Jefferson, then, Grant submits to a process in which he is conscious of his injured pride. Only when he abandons his sense of personal sacrifice and injury does he begin to make progress.

Grant says that he believes in nothing, and certainly he describes himself to Vivian as "running in place . . . unable to accept what used to be my life, unable to leave it" (102). His primary strategy for coping seems to be detached compliance. By his own admission, he merely teaches what the white folks tell him to, and he similarly follows Aunt Lou's instructions when he makes mere motions in visiting Jefferson. Vivian, however, insists that Grant do his best for Jefferson—and for her—thus forcing Grant to move to a new level of interest. All along Grant has recognized parts of himself in Jefferson, especially the futility of their positions. Now, though, Grant begins to see possibility. Grant's verbal confession that he needs Jefferson, because Jefferson represents his "need to know what to do with my life," suggests not only a reversal of roles but also an emotional breakthrough (193). Gaines will emphasize this with Grant's fight in the Rainbow Club, illustrative of his passionate commitment to Jefferson and all that he has come to represent. Provoked by the conversation of two mulatto bricklayers, this fight is Grant's physical response to racism. Grant's level of commitment has become so intense that the owner has to threaten one of the bricklayers with a gun and knock Grant unconscious to stop him.

Despite himself Grant discovers unshakable emotional ties to the people on Pichot and in Bayonne, especially Aunt Lou, Vivian, and the children. All require his service and commitment, which he often resents. Conscious of their demands, Grant asks Vivian, "What the hell do you all want from me?" (210). And while she cannot say specifically what she wants, Vivian recognizes that he has not yet given his best. Precisely what Grant is willing to give is initially both limited and measured, signified by the Westcott ruler he carries. Not simply a token of his authority, this yardstick indicates the measured gestures of Grant's existence, his controlled responses to the conditions he encounters. What Grant comes to understand is that the unspoken demands of Vivian and Aunt Lou add meaning and value to his life. Ultimately, Grant discovers that the power of love has returned him to Pichot after going to California; love ensures his reluctant instruction of Jefferson and his continuing commitment to the children he teaches. Readers witness the depth of his respect and commitment to his aunt in Grant's understanding of her unspoken demands, in his insistence upon the children's academic performance, and in his appreciation of the pastoral elements of Bayonne. Ultimately, Grant will come to fully apprehend the meaning of God and love, telling Jefferson that "God . . . makes people care for people" (223). And while he will reject Paul Bonin's compliment of his being a "great teacher," Grant shows such promise by revealing his emotions to his students (254).

While Grant is able to express his views about the world and his relation to it, Jefferson is almost entirely mute. Like Grant, Jefferson is angry, so angry, in fact, that he cannot express his rage except to turn it inward or on those who love him. Seeing Jefferson from Grant's perspective, readers have no access to his thoughts other than his expressed intention of acting like a hog. Gaines presents us with a hurt, inarticulate character absorbed in his own pain. Readers begin to witness Jefferson's changing attitude, though, when he agrees to Grant's suggestion that he show Emma respect by eating her food. But it's his diary that most fully brings to life Jefferson's character. Here, readers encounter a character who suggests the life histories of the inarticulate and unrecognized many whose labor is unstinting and unrewarded. Jefferson's simple description of beginning fieldwork when he was six years old gives readers only a glimmer of the conditions he endured. More important, though, is his recognition that he was never expected to respond to these conditions as a human being, only as a work animal. The representation of Jefferson's interior thoughts compresses in a few pages an affecting portrait of an intelligent observer sensitive to the needs of others. As the community begins sharing Jefferson's experience, he moves from his self-centeredness. Knowing that others care, Jefferson becomes stronger, setting, in the end, an example of compassionate giving. Thus, when he tells Paul to say he "walked like a man," Jefferson refers not only to his courage but his willingness to be a community hero.

Once again Gaines's women are models of commitment and caring. Both Lou and Emma have raised others' children as their own, sharing their meager livings with love and generosity. Though they don't openly ask for any reward, Lou and Emma do expect some return on their investment of time and love. Several times when she asks people to help her see Jefferson, Emma will remind them of the sacrifices she has made, suggestive of her long history of service. Just once, before she dies, she wants someone to do something for her, she says. Vivian shows similar altruistic characteristics by having violated the racial strictures of her Creole family and through her community commitment. Grant credits Vivian with his commitment to Jefferson. Certainly, she encourages his interaction, telling him that he will "do it for us." When Grant believes that his efforts are futile, saying that nothing is changing, Vivian assures him that something is. Finally, when Grant attempts to leave behind Jefferson and Vivian, he finds he cannot do so because there is nothing outside Vivian's house for him. The women, then, serve as the unshakable support of this community.

THEMATIC CONCERNS AND LITERARY DEVICES

Gaines has often said that his writing career was motivated in part by his desire to create characters absent from other novels and stories he read. Unable to find people he knew in the scarce and generally stereotyped black figures he encountered in American fiction, Gaines would create his own characters representing the truth of his experience and imagination. In so doing, he would necessarily create a fiction counter to prevailing modes, a fiction that, by virtue of its different perspective, would expose racial myths. He gives Grant Wiggins a similar task in *A Lesson Before Dying* by having him expose the "old lies" of racial mythology. Jefferson's lawyer blindly summarizes the reasoning underlying racial myths in his concluding argument to the jury. Linking Jefferson to an animal from "blackest Africa," he confidently states that Jefferson would not recognize the names of Keats, Byron, and Scott. Nor would he be able to recite a passage from the Constitution or Bill of Rights (7–8). Gaines holds the ironies of American history up before his readers, placing in the lawyer's mouth language outlining how, having denied human status to African Americans on the basis of physiological differences, legislative bodies proceeded to outlaw teaching blacks to read and write and then justified denial of political access partly on the basis of intellectual deficiencies. Grant's job, and the novel's primary theme, then, is to dispel racial myths, to disprove the lie of white superiority.

Grant's main challenge is to address the issue of manhood. He already understands that the key premise of discrimination stems from a definition of black men as "three-fifths human." After three hundred years of indoctrination, this looms as an almost insurmountable hurdle. To be a black man in the South of the 1940s seems almost impossible. Like many, Grant believes that the strongest, most ambitious have fled, leaving behind their more submissive brothers. Reviewing his own education, Grant understands that his teacher, Matthew Antoine, has believed his superiority a matter of skin color. And as he submits to routine customs emphasizing his inferior status, Grant wonders, "Do I know what a man is?" (31). Casting about for a model, Grant sees none. He rejects himself as a proper example, believing his conformity a form of cowardice. As he says to Vivian, he teaches only what the white people tell him to, nothing of pride and identity, only "reading, writing, and arithmetic" (192). Reverend Ambrose seems similarly guilty of following the direction of white people. But, as Ambrose will point out, Grant is the "gump," ignorant of people's experiences and pain (218). Grant has to see beyond surface elements before he learns to detect levels of sacrifice and achievement. And he will discover the meaning of manhood and heroism in giving of oneself. Grant will ultimately define a hero as someone motivated by love, someone who "would do anything for people . . . because it would make their lives better" (191).

Eventually Grant expresses both confidence and faith in Jefferson, believing that he can prove the lie of racial mythology. Jefferson is the only one who can prove the lie precisely because he appears so typical. Seemingly slow, barely literate, docile, and expendable, Jefferson summarizes multitudes of dispossessed and disenfranchised Americans. Mute and powerless, Jefferson has adopted a purely deterministic view of life, where nothing he does matters. Believing himself without importance, Jefferson at first appears another example of racial inferiority. Given this advantage, white money is both literally and figuratively riding on Jefferson, signaled by the bet between Henry Pichot and Louis Rougan made immediately following Jefferson's trial. Repeated references to this wager, in addition to Sheriff Guidry's periodic interrogation of Grant to ensure that he is *not* making progress with Jefferson, support the white power structure's active interest in seeing Jefferson meet his death as a "contented hog" (50). From all appearances, then, Jefferson is a sure bet—at least until Grant discovers a means of reaching him.

The solution to Grant's problem lies in the community itself, as Grant inadvertently discovers in the Rainbow Club. Hearing the two men reinact Jackie Robinson's baseball plays, Grant recalls the hope and pride a single figure can inspire, particularly when the odds are against him. Remembering the role Joe Louis's boxing victory played in his own youth, Grant involves his students in Jefferson's life, not as an object of pity, but as a subject activating their energy and effort. They will work to purchase a Christmas gift for Jefferson, and they will continue to remember him through gifts of pecans and peanuts, gifts of the land linking the children to Jefferson. The radio, too, provides a necessary connection not only because it imports the outside world but also because the community insists upon participating in this purchase. As the community, including Grant, comes to recognize itself in Jefferson, it also begins to respect his value.

Bayonne has been a community for which Grant has little hope because it has seemed impervious to change. Early in the novel, Grant will describe Bayonne as a town of six thousand, almost evenly divided between blacks and whites. Black citizens, however, can move freely only "back of town," out of white citizens' sight. Multiple instances in this novel will indicate a willful blindness on the part of whites, who choose not to see the very people who stand before them. This segregated coexistence seems both normal and desirable to white residents. But as he usually does in his fiction, Gaines dramatizes the difference between public and private social dynamics, illustrating the mutual dependence of both races and within this context the potential for change. Bayonne's public dynamic is separate and unequal, as we see in references to the limited school year for black students, the courthouse toilet facilities, the Confederate flag, and the deliberate acts of rudeness directed at African Americans. The private dynamic, on the other hand, leaves more room for negotiation, as readers see when Miss Emma insists that Henri Pichot influence his brother-in-law, Sheriff Guidry, to allow Grant's jail visits. Deliberately fingering a vein of guilt by reminding the Pichots of all she has given them, Emma demands—and receives—some recompense for her lifetime of service.

Resentful of racially imposed limits, Grant detects no changes in his community until he remains in place long enough to experience slight shifts. Once again, Gaines's fiction emulates the texture of reality, measuring social change through small, often personal alterations. As he frequently does, Gaines shows his protagonist modifying his perception and direction. Readers can trace one of Grant's most significant changes in relation to religion. He will move from his original position, where he claims not to believe in God, to a more moderate one in which he doesn't believe in the church, to a final position of defining God as love to Jefferson. His ultimate conclusion suggests a personal progression from denial to acceptance, a changed perspective from exclusion to inclusion. This pattern is reiterated in his changing attitude toward his students and Jefferson and in his tentative friendship with Paul Bonin, a white deputy.

These changes occur only after Grant sheds his anger and self-contempt. Angry, he's a poor teacher to the children and Jefferson, rude to Miss Emma and Aunt Lou, and resentful of Vivian's demands. Like a child, he cannot resolve the paradox that their spoken and unspoken demands, driving him to perform services he would rather avoid, grow from their love. All along, Grant has known that Aunt Lou and Miss Emma want someone to be proud of, someone to compensate for the missing men in their lives. But he believes himself unable to shoulder the burden of three hundred years of failure. Looking into a dark void from the door of Vivian's house, however, he sees nothing for him away from her. At this point, Grant consciously decides to shoulder the burden of personal responsibility and reconcile the advantages of his community with its disadvantages.

Gaines's use of vision as a metaphor is extensive throughout *A Lesson Before Dying*. Unlike many writers, however, Gaines will call special attention to what his characters *fail* to see. One means of pointing this out is through characters' awareness of natural beauty. When Vivian visits Grant on Pichot Plantation one Sunday morning, they joke about its "pastoral" qualities, referring to the sparse furnishings of Aunt Lou's house and the outhouse. Making fun of its limitations, they almost ignore the natural beauty of the landscape. Their subsequent lovemaking in the cane rows, however, suggests a literal and figurative intimacy with place, a new relationship underscored by Vivian's conviction that they have just conceived a child. Throughout the text, characters will call Grant's attention to what is literally before his eyes, what he doesn't see. His most direct lesson comes from Reverend Ambrose, who tells Grant that he hasn't seen Aunt Lou's suffering because he hasn't wanted to look. Grant has indulged in a form of willed blindness, but he will learn to appreciate the subtle indications of meaning. Seeing Jefferson's simple nobility rise before him, he will say, "My eyes were closed before this moment" (225). Significantly, as the time for Jefferson's execution approaches, Grant and Jefferson will both express growing appreciation for the natural life around them.

Gaines's use of natural imagery to indicate heightened vision recurs at the end of the novel. While the children kneel in their church/schoolroom awaiting news of Jefferson's execution, Grant wanders outside, wondering if life and justice are more than mere coincidence. His answer appears in a singularly beautiful image, a butterfly alighting on bull grass. The juxtaposition of something so lovely in the middle of weeds strikes Grant. He wonders, "What had brought it there?" (252). In his mind, the butterfly image, a classic literary symbol of life, the soul, or rebirth, is clearly linked to Jefferson (Cirlot, 35). Thus, following its flight out of sight, Grant believes the long wait is over for Jefferson. Underscoring this image of rebirth is the subsequent exchange Grant has with Paul Bonin. Paul's parting words, Grant's invitation for a school visit, and Paul's acceptance are indicative of a renewal of life.

Setting his novel between late fall and spring, Gaines reinforces his theme of death and rebirth. This classic literary scheme is emphasized by multiple references to the Christian calendar and to Christ. To say that Jefferson is a Christ figure may be too facile, but Gaines clearly wants readers to acknowledge certain similarities between Jefferson and Christ by placing the novel's action between Christmas and Easter. The state of Louisiana seems quite conscious of the Christian calendar. Fearful that the Roman Catholic constituency might be sensitive to having two executions before Lent, it schedules Jefferson's execution two weeks after Easter, believing this delay will dim any conscious connection between Jefferson and Christ. Ironically, the state schedules all executions between noon and three on Fridays to emulate the time of Christ's execution. Gaines stimulates readers' association of Christ with Jefferson by having Jefferson ask Grant if Christmas was "when He born or . . . when He died?" (138). Another inescapable comparison occurs during the school nativity play. Dressed in the denim work clothes of the poor, Mary will receive the pennies offered by the Wise Men, surprised that they address her infant as "Savior" (150). Her comment reminds readers of the humble origins of Christ and the sacrifical nature of his life and death. Resisting the idea of being a sacrificial hero, Jefferson asks Grant, "Who ever car'd my cross?" (224). Believing himself someone who "never had nothing," Jefferson naturally struggles with the idea that he must now be "better" than others (222).

But whatever touches him—whether Grant's instruction about the nature of racial myths, Emma's expressions of love, or his own discovery of voice—leaves its effect, and thus Jefferson finds in himself the courage to face his own mortality. Grant will remark on his growth by noting Jefferson's physical stance, "big and tall," at their last meeting (225). That Jefferson has risen to be a hero to his community is signaled by their insistence on paying their respect both in the form of visits before he dies and in their refusal to work on the day of execution. This last gesture ensures that the white community, which might prefer to ignore the execution, feels its impact. A demonstration of pride and solidarity, this communal act provides ample evidence of Jefferson's lasting effect. Having walked to his death as "the bravest man in that room," Jefferson has begun to change the lives of those around him (256). And Paul Bonin's promise to tell Grant's students of Jefferson's courage suggests his continuing presence in the life of Bayonne.

A FEMINIST READING

Given Gaines's focus on male characters and his recurring theme of manhood, the feminine element of his novels might easily be overlooked. A feminist reading of *A Lesson Before Dying*, however, is certainly possible, and it offers readers an opportunity to examine more closely the role of women and their values in Gaines's world. What, then, is a "feminist" reading? Since its emergence as a critical lens in the 1970s, feminist literary criticism has developed in a variety of ways mentioned in the alternative reading of *Catherine Carmier*. Drawing upon historical and Marxist theory, British feminist theory directs readers' interest in social change through engagement with historical process. Gaines's fiction, with its drama evolving from the conflict of change, lends itself to this kind of reading, and thus one feminist reading of *A Lesson Before Dying* might look closely at the role of feminine values with respect to social change.

Embodying the history of Pichot Plantation, Emma and Lou have accepted their roles as cook and laundress, raised others' children, faithfully attended church, and remained silent. To all outward appearances, they conform to sexual and racial stereotypes as nurturing, submissive female figures. Grant, however, describes these women in terms of "stone," "oak," and "cypress," indicative of their solidity and permanence. Later, he will use "boulder" in recognition of their immense

strength and power. These women wield primarily silent power, illus-
trated by Grant's consciousness of Aunt Lou's meaningful looks, but they
also know how to speak. Both will claim a hearing in inescapable terms.
Still, their characters appear largely secondary in the construction of the
novel. But like many elements of Gaines's fiction, the more important
elements are the unspoken and unseen. A feminist reading of this book
will emphasize the women's roles as revolutionaries.

The seeds of revolution have been planted in Grant as ideas. Lou insists
that Grant learn everything he can from Matthew Antoine and promises
him other, presumably more knowlegeable, teachers. She helps him to create a positive self-image by excusing him from using Pichot's back door,
and she willingly sacrifices for Grant's university education. In short, she
raises Grant not simply as someone to break racial stereotypes but someone who challenges it by his very presence in the community. Grant's
awareness of his role as challenger is frequently expressed by his dilemma
over acting like a true teacher, or the "nigger that [he] was supposed to
be," a dilemma vividly expressed by his conscious use of grammar and his
significant pauses before adding "sir" while addressing white men (47).
Emma and Lou also act in concert to make Grant visit Jefferson, and they
keep him at it, playing on the sense of duty they instilled. Most of their co-
ercion is quiet, but Aunt Lou remains adamant that Grant will visit Jefferson, teach Jefferson his value as a man, and not quit until the very end.
Grant will try to argue, sulk, and avoid contact with both women, but he
cannot escape them.

Nor can he convince Vivian to simply run away with him from the
weight of his responsibility. When Gaines created Vivian as a married
Roman Catholic mother of two in 1940's Louisiana, he effectively chained
her to her community. Women do not typically write divorce law, especially not in Louisiana, which based its laws on Napoleonic code. Louisiana legally termed husbands "lord and master" of their homes, wives,
and children. Thus, Vivian's husband, despite having deserted his family, has legal precedence over her. Vivian will tell Grant that one condition of her husband's agreeing to a divorce is that she remain in
Bayonne. The implication of his condition is that if Grant wants to marry
her, they must stay in the community. But she has other reasons for
staying, not the least of which is her being the sole support of her two
children. Apart from these constraints on her movement, Vivian has already shown her commitment to the community as a whole by rejecting
her Creole family's belief in its racial superiority. Choosing family exile
over racism, Vivian demonstrates the strength of her morality. And she

further demonstrates it by encouraging Grant to visit Jefferson. When she tells him to teach Jefferson "for us," she may mean the two of them, but Vivian may also mean the community (32). The depth of Vivian's commitment surfaces at regular intervals in *A Lesson Before Dying*, primarily in her refusal to run away with Grant. Like Aunt Lou, Vivian wants a man to stand up for himself and for others, she wants a man brave enough to give his best, and she is strong enough to show the way. Thus, her presence in the novel is more propelling than merely supportive. Vivian's role is to make Grant act beyond his own self-perceived limits.

One historic measure of manhood has always been sexual prowess. Gaines will employ this metaphor throughout *A Lesson Before Dying*, and he will imbue it with a different meaning. Grant would like to believe his physical engagement with Vivian is evidence of his love and commitment. When his sexual performance falters after frustrating sessions with Jefferson, Grant is embarrassed, expressing his sensitivity by saying that things had not been going well lately. His belief that his manhood and sexuality are one and the same is directly contradicted by Vivian in their climactic argument. Vivian contends that sex is not enough, certainly not evidence of Grant's best effort, his best expression of himself. She insists that his "best" involves "consideration," implying action which takes others into account (210).

These values clash directly with those of the white establishment, particularly with reference to its treatment of black citizens. Taking them into account is something whites simply refused to do. Having created the myth of racial superiority and perpetuated its "truth" by rigging the educational and legal system, whites sustain the illusion of their right to power. Represented by Pichot the landowner, Rougan the banker, and Guidry the sheriff, Bayonne's power is all white and all male; its values tend to be active, blunt, and authoritative. These characters say they know what happened, and they are convinced of their rightness. Grant, however, knows that there is another story, another set of values, such as self-abnegation, sacrifice, and silence often defined as "feminine." Living in a culture that has systematically denied manhood to black males, Grant must redefine manhood in terms of what is both understandable and possible to achieve. He does this by embracing the feminine. As Grant's understanding and description of heroic action sharpen, his language becomes distinctly feminine, with its emphasis on love and willing self-sacrifice. Rather than reverse the meaning of heroism, though, Grant co-opts it and gives it a more sustaining quality.

Thus, *A Lesson Before Dying* works to redefine manhood in terms of personal commitment and sacrifice. Though perhaps implicit in heroism, these terms are too often lost in the bombast of achievement. Gaines, however, shifts reader attention from epic action to domestic. Focusing on the ordinary, he points readers toward the extraordinary acts of courage required of those willing to remain in place to fight for change. The social revolutions Ernest Gaines writes about are individual and yet representative. At the very center of these revolutions are female characters who, like boulders, remain firm and immovable. From them emanate the moral actions his male characters reluctantly assume.

9

The Short Stories: *Bloodline*
(1968)

Throughout his career, Ernest Gaines has said that he writes about "survival with sanity and love and sense of responsibility, and getting up and trying all over again not only for one's self but mankind" (Lowe, 96). Nowhere is his concern more forcefully evident than in his collected short stories, *Bloodline*. Each story offers an ever-widening perspective of the meaning of manhood, a term readers should understand as being more inclusive than gendered. To Gaines, manliness means "that moment when . . . dignity demands that you act," not merely for one's own sake but for the sake of others (242). Each of the first four stories in *Bloodline* takes its protagonist on a journey of discovery. As they move out into an increasingly complex world, Gaines's characters will learn how to interpret the various signs they encounter and how to act with dignity within a culture that denies them human value. The final story, "Just Like a Tree," offers, through its multiple narrators, a community commentary on the nature of individual and social change.

Although Gaines had begun writing the five stories that comprise *Bloodline* before 1959, he ultimately unified them before the book's publication in 1968. Three of this collection's stories, "A Long Day in November," "The Sky Is Gray," and "Just Like a Tree," had already appeared in journals. Noting a common theme and a chronological progression between "Day" and "Sky," Gaines went on to create two more stories of young manhood. Similar to Faulkner's *Go Down, Moses*, Gaines crafted his stories to reflect the individual and social forces shaping human behavior. Presenting a representative cross section of ages and experiences, Gaines guides readers on the problematic journey to black manhood. Taken singly, each story offers a complete fictional experience, thus basically limiting critical discussion to its main conflict. Read together as a novel, the stories in *Bloodline* give readers a comprehensive view of not only the various obstacles and choices individuals must make but also how these choices affect us all.

"A LONG DAY IN NOVEMBER"

"A Long Day in November" traces an eventful day in the life of its six-year-old narrator, Sonny Howard. During this day, Sonny will watch his parents, Amy and Eddie, separate—apparently over a car but really about accepting responsibility—and then reunite when they find a means of reconciling their differences. Sonny's sensory responses to dreams, people, and events give his story both immediacy and authenticity. Gaines's use of time emulates a child's sense of time, when length and distance are relative to event. Thus, the day is long, when in fact November days are relatively short, but long because Sonny's apprehension of each episode captivates his full attention. And the distance to his grandmother Rachel's house seems further than it is because of his size and reluctance to leave his own home. The story begins with Sonny's early morning awakening—part of his ongoing toilet training—and ends with his late night return to bed. In between rising and falling asleep, Sonny experiences life-altering shifts in behavior, particularly his father's redefinition of manhood.

The story's central conflict arises between Amy and Eddie. A field hand, Eddie has purchased an old car with his wife's financial assistance. He has fallen in love with the car, finding in it an expression of physical freedom he has never experienced. And his devotion to its maintenance as well as time spent driving it have made him an absentee husband and father. Now tired of her husband's absenteeism, Amy has decided to leave him. Early in the morning, she and Sonny pack and walk to her mother's home in the quarters.

At her mother's house, more issues emerge, though Sonny doesn't recognize them as such. Amy's mother, Rachel, has always disliked Eddie because, to her mind, he lacks an essential ingredient of manhood: a sense of personal responsibility. Eddie's relationship to his car proves her point: "When they got their troubles, they come running to the womenfolks. When they ain't got no troubles and when their pockets full of money, they run jump in the car" (18). According to Rachel, Eddie is like every other man in and around Bayonne, because he "don't care for nobody, 'cluding himself" (19). This apparent self-centeredness—which is in reality a lack of self-value and self-respect—make Eddie worthless in Rachel's book.

Another factor plays a lesser role in her dislike of Eddie, and that is his color. Rachel consistently characterizes Eddie by his color, referring to him as "yellow" (18) or "mariny" (31), suggesting half-white status. Amy appears to be lighter and thus holds higher status, as her mother reminds her, recalling her "Long silky curls" (19). As the prettiest girl on the plantation with her light skin, Amy might have had her choice of the most eligible man available, someone who would support her in comfort. Instead, she has married a field hand whose reliability is questionable and whose earning ability is marginal. Now she faces a choice of either finding another man or cutting cane to support herself and Sonny. To Rachel, cutting cane is beneath Amy's status. But Amy is a woman who has clearly inherited a good deal of her mother's considerable strength and integrity. Having made her own selection in Eddie, she's not about to let her mother run her life. She refuses to accept the easy arrangement Rachel orchestrates with Freddie Jackson, a former and persistent suitor. After all, she still loves Eddie Howard.

Sonny witnesses events that he cannot quite grasp, and this gap provides a good portion of the story's comedy. Still, he proves an accurate reporter when Eddie, enraged that Rachel is arranging a union between Amy and Freddie Jackson, goes first to the preacher, whose advice is worthless, and then to Madame Toussaint, resident wise woman and advisor. The advice Madame Toussaint gives is for Eddie to burn his car, an idea that he strongly resists. But when Amy agrees to return home if he does, Eddie arranges to fetch the car. He sets fire to it with the entire plantation as witness. Afterward, the Howards return to their own home, where Amy and Eddie resolve the real issue troubling their marriage. Having proven that he values Amy above the vehicle and having made a public display of his values, Eddie must also illustrate his personal commitment to family, especially to his son.

Throughout the day, and especially in school, Sonny has been unprepared. Gaines employs the act of learning to read as a significant metaphor in this story, associating the act with an ability to correctly interpret signs (Byerman, *Fingering the Jagged Edge*, 74). A beginning reader, Sonny needs practice, which Amy has usually supervised. In its absence, he performs poorly in class, wetting his pants in his anxiety and thus becoming the target of teasing. While his teacher correctly interprets Sonny's mishap as a sign of trouble at home, the children read this as a mark of his immaturity. At stake is Sonny's reputation as a baby or as a "man." His teacher has sent a note to the Howards requesting a school visit. Eddie, uncomfortable in the schoolroom, has let Amy assume the chore of guiding Sonny's reading practice. Now Amy proposes that they share this responsibility for their son's education, alternating nights of helping Sonny read. To Amy, it's time for Eddie to learn how to act around a schoolroom, how to guide his son's education.

Gaines's story gives us a vivid sense of a child's response to his world. Everywhere, Sonny reports on smells, colors, sounds, and textures. Simple acts, like having a bowel movement or using a fork, hold importance for Sonny because they mark steps toward independence, transforming him from a baby into a man. Like all children, Sonny is eager to participate in his world, his curiosity stimulated by the new events of his day. And like all children, Sonny fails to fully comprehend both the signs and the language of his physical experience, though he has a child's intuitive sense of people.

Eddie Howard is not the model of manhood either Amy or Rachel admires, for when he purchases physical independence in the car, he abandons his responsibilities. Free to roam after work, Eddie expects Amy to remain at home, tend to Sonny, and welcome him whenever he appears. To Eddie, love seems to mean physical contact. Amy knows that genuine love goes much further, and she requires proof. In agreeing to burn his car for Amy, Eddie announces to the community a degree of personal sacrifice he has never fathomed, and with this gesture, he becomes—even to the grudging Rachel—"a man after all" (71).

This is a lovely story, poignant and comic, imbued with implications yet simple enough for children to enjoy. In fact, Gaines published this story separately for children in 1971. Young readers might be particularly taken with Sonny's enjoyment of smells, textures, and colors, his physical response to the world. With its simple vocabulary, "A Long Day in November" evokes another time and place, far removed from technology and the fast pace of the urban scene. These seemingly simple rhythms, however, are rich in implication. Older readers will find a much more sophisticated subtext, related through Sonny's remembered sounds and actions, his innocent reportage of conversations, and his attention to adult actions.

Stories depend more on conflict than character, their themes emerging from the opposition of forces. Gaines sets the major theme of manhood early in this particular story, in the collection as a whole, and in the lives of his characters, illustrating that men are made; they don't simply develop by themselves. When Amy and Eddie struggle with one another, they fight over more than a car. They are really struggling with how to respect and treat one another. Gaines emphasizes this by having Eddie seek advice from Madame Toussaint. As the resident sage, she seems to know the truth about what is going on. She corrects Eddie's exaggerated version of events and demands her price despite his protestations. Thinking he can get secondhand advice for free, Eddie seeks out two men friends who have gone to Madame Toussaint with marital difficulties. Each has been told to take a specific action, and both have been pleased with the result. Of course, they wouldn't need to ask Madame Toussaint if they had talked to their wives; even Madame Toussaint knows this. When Eddie returns with a borrowed three dollars to pay Madame Toussaint and then wants to argue with her, she stops him, saying men "never know how a woman feels because you never ask how she feels" (61). Implicit in her statement are several possibilities: men aren't curious about how women feel, they don't value the feelings of women, and they are oblivious to women's feelings. All point to the devaluation of women's feelings, a social practice we also see in this story when men are belittled for showing their emotions. At this point, Gaines injects an often ignored element of manhood: caring about how others feel. He reinforces this by creating the character of Bill. One of the older boys at school, Bill is a nurturing figure, helping Miss Hebert, the teacher, by assisting her with the younger children. He shows understanding and kindness to Sonny, protecting him from the taunts of older children, and inspires Sonny's admiration.

"A Long Day in November" closes with Amy's insistence that Eddie beat her because she doesn't want him to be "the laughingstock of the plantation" (75). The public valuation of manhood as being unemotional and oblivious to women except as sexual objects remains, though personal relations are conducted on a different scale. Amy preserves Eddie's public male status, even as she assigns him an important task outside the stereotypical male arena. Tomorrow, he will take Sonny to school to discuss his reading with Miss Hebert. Eddie's discomfort in such a situation is dismissed when she states that it's time for him to learn how to act in such a place. He doesn't argue with her, nor does he protest supervising Sonny's prayers despite the fact that he says no prayers of

his own. The story moves full circle to Sonny's freely associated summary of his day, including his resolve not to wet himself any longer. He
has absorbed a good deal of knowledge about himself and others. As he
falls asleep in the warm cave of his bedclothes listening to the rhythmic
screech of bedsprings, Sonny is aware only of the peace and security the
noise implies.

"THE SKY IS GRAY"

"The Sky Is Gray" is one of Gaines's most frequently anthologized
stories for good reason. By recapitulating a day's events in the life of its
eight-year-old protagonist and narrator, James, Gaines gives readers a
vivid sense of the struggle for dignity the poor encounter on a daily
basis. The story's events center on a trip to the dentist, but the conflict
is over learning to cope with a social system designed to deny self-esteem
while maintaining self-respect. For James, there's no time for childhood.
The oldest of four children in a family whose father has been drafted by
the U.S. Army, James finds himself "the man" of the family and a "sam-
ple" [example] to his younger siblings. His father's absence has thrust
the entire family to a precarious financial edge and has forced James to
new levels of stoicism: "I can't never be scared and I can't ever cry" (84),
he says. For weeks he has tried to ignore the pain of his toothache, not
because he's afraid of the dentist but because he understands that the
family cannot afford to have it pulled. He owes his courageous attitude
in large part to his strong mother, Octavia.

Resolute, erect, smart, and proud, Octavia has managed to feed a family of six as a field-worker without her husband's earnings. More important to her, however, is teaching her son to comport himself in a
manner that will allow him to survive with dignity. To this end, Octavia
has instructed James with a strict discipline, making him take actions
against his will. Her insistence on James's killing a trapped cardinal
seems cruel, and her beating when he resists seems unreasonable. But
James, with the assistance of his aunt and godfather, comes to understand his mother's action as a necessary lesson in survival: "Suppose she
had to go away like Daddy went away? Then who was go'n to look after
us" (90). While Auntie insists that Octavia explain her reasons for forcing
James to act, Octavia remains silent, forcing James to begin learning to
interpret actions for himself (Byerman, *Fingering the Jagged Edge*, 76). In
any case, just how does one explain the kinds of unspoken rules, restric-

tions and insults James will encounter on a daily basis because of his race?

When the bus stops for James and Octavia, they move toward the rear, behind the sign noting "Colored," though only one seat remains while there are many unoccupied seats in the "White" section. This is a rare trip for James, one taking him from the known world of the plantation to a larger, more alien space. When they arrive in Bayonne, James passes the school where white children play and a cafe he cannot enter. Nothing in Bayonne is freely open to James and Octavia, even the sidewalks. Gaines's story plays on the irony of James's father defending his country while his family lives in a state that ignores civil rights for African Americans by having James note the difference in the flags waving over the courthouse and his school: "This one here ain't got but a handful of stars. One at school got a big pile of stars—one for every state."(93). As they move through Bayonne, James notes additional places he cannot enter. Even at the dentist's office they must wait in a segregated section. Bayonne is for whites. Black people may enter selected stores only to purchase items, as Octavia illustrates when she pretends to test ax handles so that her child can get warm. For food, they must walk to "back of town," where whites don't deign to eat.

Learning to interpret human actions remains at the thematic center of this story, as we see in the dentist's office. A cross section of poor people wait for Dr. Bassett, a dentist whose skills are so inferior that he takes black patients. These include a preacher and a young man reading a book. James is quite taken with the young man because he wears a suit and "looks like a teacher or somebody that goes to college" (95). This young man infuriates the preacher and others by asking for proof, evidence that what they believe is grounded in fact, not hearsay. He asks, "What do words like Freedom, Liberty, God, White, Colored mean?" (97), thus challenging social conditions and the very language used to describe reality. During his debate with waiting people, the young man points out "Citizens have certain rights. Name me one right that you have. One right, granted by the Constitution, that you can exercise in Bayonne" (101). The feeble response that "Things changing" (101) proves the young man's point: things are changing only because of the courage to challenge the *status quo*. The young man's arguments spark violence from the preacher, who strikes out in frustration and fear because he cannot effectively disprove the young man's logic, and both the logic and language might inspire white reprisals that would endanger the black community. Equally important, the young man's statements inspire sadness in a lady sitting across from James and Octavia because in his application of strict logic, the young man has apparently "Done forgot the heart absolutely" (192). But the young man shows respect for her position by agreeing that he hopes everyone doesn't become like him. He wants people to have faith in "something definitely that they can lean on" (102).

That faith, for James and Octavia, gets unexpected support from a kind couple. Throughout this day the weather has become increasingly chilly, and both James and Octavia have thin protection from the cold. When they are forced back to the streets for another hour during lunch, the cold, which has turned to sleet, becomes numbing, especially when combined with their hunger. Another long walk takes them back of town, where Octavia purchases a glass of milk and cookies for James and a cup of coffee for herself at the price of their return bus ticket. Now, they will have to walk home. But on their way back to town, they are stopped by an elderly white woman named Helena, who asks about whether they have eaten and their afternoon plans. As the dialogue suggests, this character has seen Octavia and James earlier, surmised their position, fixed food for them, and has gone outside to find them. Her persistence has paid off, though she almost loses them to Octavia's pride. In offering them food, she seems to be giving charity, and Octavia is not one to take something for nothing. But Helena quickly recognizes Octavia's position, and shows her respect by saying that James will have to work for their food. When Octavia says that James will move the garbage cans for free, Helena counters with "Not unless you eat. . . . I'm old, but I have my pride, too, you know" (113). Later, these women will struggle over a piece of salt meat, as Helena will try to be generous, and Octavia will refuse her measure, insisting that she weigh the pork and adjust the measure. As she pays for her purchase, Octavia says, "Your kindness will never be forgotten" (117). This statement of fact is not an expression of gratitude but rather a recognition of action.

"The Sky Is Gray" rings with autobiographical truths recalling Gaines's Aunt Augusteen, his redoubtable mother, and a simple gesture of human kindness. But the story moves well beyond autobiography into art. With remarkable economy, Gaines evokes an entire region and era through describing Bayonne. This is not a place of childhood myth, full of warmth and remembered play. Rather, it is a sometimes cold and bewildering obstacle course, particularly for a young black male. Bayonne does not welcome James and Octavia. It maintains a vigilance, waiting for them to spend whatever money they have and then leave. For James to attain manhood with a measure of dignity and self-pride in such an environment becomes another—perhaps the principal—challenge for Octavia. Her constant supervision of James's behavior, including reminders to wipe his nose and keep his collar down, are lessons in dignity. As she reminds him in the last line of the story, "You not a bum, . . . You a man" (117).

The story's title sets its mood and introduces the idea of color and meaning. Literally, "gray" describes the cold, wet weather reflecting the actual season and the family's mood. Reduced to a dull cycle of work and rest, family life has been drained of its color by the sheer effort to survive. James's observation about the sky's color prepares readers for the waiting room discussion when the young man claims that wind is pink and grass black. In drawing attention to the association of color and meaning as well as the interpretation of meaning, the young man seems to confuse everyone. People often accept language at face value, never asking why a word means what it means. In asking what "black" means, he points out that we believe it to mean something specific merely on the basis of convention. What basis in fact does that meaning actually have? In other words, the young man is challenging how we view reality and how we determine truth. In believing merely what we are told, in not challenging received wisdom, we drain language of its very meaning, he maintains. Only action has any meaning. James finds this character admirable in every respect and hopes he'll grow up to become someone like him.

"THREE MEN"

Gaines dramatically continues his exploration of manhood in "Three Men." By now, readers of the collection may recognize some common factors. First, there is the progression of ages of his different protagonists. With Proctor Lewis of "Three Men," Gaines moves into early adulthood. Again the father is absent, though a substitute figure will appear. And the environment itself plays another important role. This time cold weather doesn't set the story's mood. A grim jail cell does. Nineteen-year-old Proctor Lewis has defended himself in a fight, accidentally killing his opponent. Rather than wait for the law to come after him, he has turned himself in, confident that Roger Medlow, an important local white man, will arrange his release. Lewis is placed in a cell with Munford Bazille, an older man who has discovered the true price of not accepting the responsibility for his actions. During their night in jail, Munford will try to teach Lewis the personally fatal result of taking actions without considering their full consequences.

"Three Men" depends in large part on setting and situation. Placing his action inside a jail, Gaines focuses reader attention on a bleak but intimate space occupied by men who share a common fate dictated by gender and race. Munford, Hattie, and Proctor apparently have little in common; yet each has committed a crime of passion. Hattie has performed a sex act on another man in a movie theatre, Munford has choked someone, and Proctor has murdered a man named Bayou in a fight over a woman. Still, as Munford assures Proctor, "A nigger ain't nobody" and thus their crimes have no meaning (136). The only importance of black men, as far as Munford can see, is in defining what white men apparently are not. White men, he asserts, "see us and know what they ain't" (138). But he also concludes that simply having black men in jail doesn't make a man any more than having women, fighting with other men, or killing others. Animals, after all, perform those actions. Being a man, then, involves something more, and that something includes taking responsibility for one's actions. It ultimately comes to mean serving time in prison instead of supporting white expectations, instead of killing more black men. Munford's description of how the culture deprives black men of their manhood is both graphic and comic as his folk story details culture's multiple assaults on black manhood. It's also quite serious. His experience in killing his own has proven his point: "they grow niggers just to be killed, and they grow people like you to kill 'em. That's all part of the—the culture" (142). Having imparted this advice, Munford tips his hat to Proctor and calls a guard to release him.

Throughout the story, Proctor has assumed that he will not serve any time. In fact, he may never even have to go to trial. Young and strong, he fears being caged, but beyond this, he feels self-righteous. He didn't mean to kill anyone, didn't carry a weapon, and was only acting in self-defense. At the same time, he feels badly that he has killed, and that he was angry at his victim. Munford's words make him think through what calling for Roger Medlow's help will mean. And as he sifts through his confused feelings, he attempts to be completely truthful. Moving aside all of his rationalizations, Proctor finally concludes that he hasn't loved anyone since his mother died. Now he wishes that he knew a good person to be a model for him.

That men and women are expected to respond differently to events is particularly emphasized through the contrast of Munford's character with Hattie's. Munford describes Hattie as a "woman" (127) made by a culture that systematically deprives him of manhood from infancy. The choices for black men, according to Munford, are to either become like Hattie, a woman, or like Munford, a "beast" (140), uncaring to the point of becoming murderous. Hattie's sympathy, his explicit show of emotions, and his fear of violence combine to make him a "freak" in Proctor's eyes (133). Proctor's repeated refrain in regard to this character is "I didn't want to have nothing to do with that freak" (145). But if Munford serves as an unexpected father figure, Hattie becomes Proctor's unwitting and disregarded "mother." Ultimately, Proctor takes Munford's advice—accepting responsibility for personal acts—and emulates Hattie's actions—giving comfort. Unlike Hattie, however, he doesn't merely attempt to soothe. Instead, he attempts to teach the boy a combination of acceptance and care imbued with faith in something beyond himself.

He becomes an unwilling model for his fourteen-year-old cellmate, who has been arrested, beaten, and thrown into the cell with Hattie and Proctor. Proctor doesn't come to this decision easily. First, he reviews the motions he knows best—insults, calls for help, physical violence—and rejects all to accept punishment for his crime. He will serve his sentence, even if Medlow comes for him, because he now wants "to stand" (152) instead of pretending to ignore the violence done to black men. In short, Proctor recognizes how resistance affirms the value of his life. Having reached this decision, he now feels "so good I wanted to sing" (152). Now he can become a father to the boy, teaching him how to be a man. This lesson focuses on mutual respect and nurturing. Telling the boy that the only way he will be able to take the beatings he knows will come, Proctor asks for the boy's prayers—despite the fact that he doesn't believe in God. Asking for the prayers brings him from a sense of isolation and helplessness to a sense of purpose (Byerman, *Fingering the Jagged Edge*, 82). Then he performs two actions that he once would have believed too feminine for a man: he washes the boy's bruises and their shirts. These actions suggest a redefinition of manhood, one far more complex than his earlier, simplistic notions.

It would be easy for Gaines to slip into stereotype in his story. In fact, the surface features of his characters in "Three Men" can easily be read at face value, with little regard for Gaines's careful thematic development. Looking closer, readers can see that Gaines balances brutal deputy T. J. with a kinder Paul. And he treats the occupants of the jail cell with much the same fairness. Readers should remember that Proctor's point of view, which controls this story, is accurate only up to a point. He has viewed reality from his limited perspective, rationalizing and justifying his behavior, wanting to believe whatever seems most convenient for him. In general, Proctor is a reliable narrator, one readers can believe. But in having him go through his "truths," and in recognizing them for the convenient screens they are, Gaines makes Proctor even more reliable. Proctor must come to see that he may never have loved anyone because genuine love involves self-sacrifice, something he has been unwilling to accept. Further, he must not simply blame white people, though he tries this argument, too. Blaming others—however justifiable—is another evasion of personal accountability. In the end, he claims to feel some kind of love for this boy, whose own parents failed to assume responsibility for their child, and he tries to pass on, not only through words but actions, the most important lessons of his life. In the end, Proctor's uncertainty is far more realistic than his earlier, confident claims.

"BLOODLINE"

The collection's title story, "Bloodline," appears after "Three Men." Told from the point of view of seventy-year-old Felix, a semiretired field hand on the Laurent Plantation, "Bloodline" treats in a comic fashion our common inheritance. The story focuses on the maneuvers between white plantation owner Frank Laurent and his half-black nephew, Copper, to discuss Copper's birthright. Now in his late sixties, Frank is the last of his immediate line. Ailing after several heart attacks, he plans to leave his plantation to a niece in nearby Bayonne. Copper, Frank's brother Walter's son, has returned from the North, where he has been living. Calling himself General Christian Laurent, Copper wants to be recognized as a family member. Moreover, he believes that he ought to inherit the property. Initially, the struggle between the two men will focus on which door he may enter the big house.

The old plantation world of the slave era is giving way to another social order, as everyone on the plantation recognizes. Still, most of those hands remaining on the plantation seem to conform to the ways of the past, particularly Felix and Amalia. As Frank's contemporaries, they have lived on the plantation all their lives and have both respect and affection for him. Amalia, who is Copper's aunt on his mother's side, continues to serve as companion and nurse to Frank despite her own frailty. Wearing the head rag that signified house servants during slavery, she always enters the house by the back door. Being a faithful servant, however, doesn't blind her to the truth. With the simple statement that Copper is "Us nephew," she asserts her kinship with Frank (175). Felix, who is more physically active, also plays his expected role. Now retired from fieldwork, he sharpens old tools daily, just in case they are ever needed again and because he measures his personal worth through work. These hand tools, so essential before a technological revolution in farming, suggest his connection to a past, though not necessarily one he misses. Felix respects Frank, despite his autocratic behavior. He both accepts and subverts Frank's displaced anger and his high-handed commands with the ironic response "You the authority" (184). Authority is, in fact, the issue in question.

Images of authority dominate the Laurent home, especially its living room which features pictures of soldiers everywhere. On the mantelpiece is a painting of Walter on his stallion, significantly named Black Terror. As Felix recalls Walter's violence, his unquestioned command of people and place, and his heedless actions, he remembers Walter's death, in which the positions depicted in the painting are reversed. Walter is dragged to his death by Black Terror, suggestive of justice, even retribution. Recalling his death, Felix sees not Walter, but Copper and concludes that Copper and Walter are "the same two" (193). Both father and son seem to embody violent authority and thus threaten the plantation community. Felix and Amalia fear the possible conflict between the uncompromising Copper and his Uncle Frank.

As the last of the Laurents, Frank has been both perpetuator and victim of a social system in which he has inherited both privilege and responsibility. He has given his life to the plantation, but instead of having a peaceful old age, he discovers himself in the middle of a social revolution. Throughout the story, Gaines will contrast Frank with his brother, Walter. Together they represent both sides of slaveholders, one suggesting benevolent paternalism and the other high-handed appropriation and ruthlessness. Frank believes that he truly cares about black plantation residents, allowing people to live on the plantation rent free and seeing that some basic needs are met. But he never comprehends the price of his affection. In return for his favors and now nonexistent protection, he expects unquestioning obedience. Walter has played a different role: autocratic, violent, and reckless. Apparently the family profligate, he has spawned numerous half-caste children, indicated by the story's dialogue and supported by the presence of the yellow Dee-Dee in the kitchen. Walter's violent death suggests the passing of the physical brutality once used to maintain authority. Frank's gentler approach has sparked respect, mostly because he has attempted to compensate for his brother's excesses. Despite his kinder approach, he threatens a return to past methods when he feels thwarted, his language suggesting nostalgia for immediate compliance. Felix knows that Frank and Walter share autocratic natures, a commanding demeanor reflected in Copper. So the struggle between the uncle and nephew isn't so much about differences as about likeness. Frank orders that Copper come to him and enter the house through the back door. Copper refuses. In time-honored fashion, Frank resorts to force, sending two strong men after Copper. When Copper returns these two in chains, Frank sends six, who are easily defeated. Who is in charge, he wonders.

Despite his claims to authority, Frank understands that his is diminished. Old and ill, he's entirely dependent upon the kindness of Felix and especially Amalia. But though he calls Amalia a "lady," and allows her to sit in the library, he cannot allow her to enter the house through the front door. Frank honestly believes that in preserving the customs of the past, he somehow protects everyone. And when his observance of "the rules" comes into question, he avoids responsibility by claiming that he didn't make them. These "rules" govern social custom, and these "rules" generally give license to one race at the expense of another, though Frank seems selectively blind to this. Change will come, as Frank recognizes, but he won't initiate it. When he realizes that Copper has defeated him, Frank appears to accept his defeat with the grace of a true gentleman. He meets Copper at Amalia's house.

Felix provides readers with a minute description of the customs both men observe when they meet. Copper refuses to descend the steps and meet Frank at the car, he calls Frank "Uncle," invites him to sit, and offers him something to drink, treating Frank with the perfect courtesy of equals. When Copper finishes dressing in his military attire and rejoins Frank on the porch, he takes the dominant position by sitting on the bannister. Then uncle and nephew play a game, each maneuvering for advantage. Copper asks for his birthright, one he cannot claim, according to Frank, because his mother was black. But that can't stop him from claiming it in the future, he says, and he has an army of people who have been treated just as he was behind him, maybe not in physical fact but in the spiritual sense.

In section 11, "Bloodline" will reach its climax, becoming much more direct, as Copper turns Frank's use of language on him. First he ques-

tions just how long Frank has called black males "men," and then he
lands on the contradiction implicit in Frank's accusing Copper of using
"chains and sticks" (209) to bring about change. Just who has invented
and employed violent methods against whom, he asks. Who originated
lynching and sexual mutilation? Beyond sheer force, white men created
the biased law. "It was written by you for you and your kind, and any
man who was not of your kind had to break it sooner or later" (209).
This key section will summarize relations between races, as Copper recalls history and his response to events in his life. During this summa-
tion, Frank listens, his emotions conveyed through his cane, which bears
more and more pressure as he recognizes the truth of Copper's statement, and his hand over his weak heart, implying emotional damage.
Similarly, Copper will touch his head, signifying psychological damage.
Plantation residents consider him "insane" for making his claims. But
Felix perceptively characterizes this action as "listening to something far
off" (208), suggestive of Copper's listening to voices others cannot yet
hear. Frank's claim that his suffering has been equal to Copper's might
sound hollow, but his statement that neither he nor Copper can change
the rules "singly" (216) bears considerable truth. Both sides need to work
together. Despite his apparently conciliatory action, Frank's adherence
to the rules that he inherited and will continue to enforce suggests his
attachment to a dead past. In the end, Copper leaves, promising a return
and a change that will allow Amalia big-house entry through the front
door. Copper's brisk, military exit suggests not a retreat but a strategic
withdrawal.

In several respects, "Bloodline" recalls Faulkner's story "Was," where
the slave Terrell leads his half-brothers, Buck and Buddy McCaslin, on
a ritualized chase to a neighboring plantation and proceeds to manipulate everyone to win his woman. Issues of kinship, birthright, time, and
justice permeate Faulkner's story, just as they do in Gaines's, and both
stories use comedy as an effective means of dramatizing these themes.
Faulkner's story, however, retains its comic tone to the end, while
Gaines's drops the attitude to drive home his theme. In placing aside his
comic mask, Gaines deepens the impact of his theme, asking readers to
dwell on the story's controlling question. Given the history of race relations in this country, what is our birthright, and how do we redress
the wrongs inflicted throughout the years? "Bloodline" goes beyond the
immediate relationship between Frank and Copper to embrace our common human kinship.

"JUST LIKE A TREE"

"Just Like a Tree," the collection's concluding story, takes its title and controlling metaphor from a Negro spiritual that begins with the line, "I shall not be moved" (221). Aunt Fe, one of the oldest remaining residents on the Duvall Plantation, is about to be taken north by her niece, Louise, and her husband, James. A nearby bombing to discourage civil rights activities has prompted Louise's decision. As Aunt Fe's only living relative, Louise feels responsible for her safety. The story takes place in Fe's home during a community farewell in Fe's honor.

Told from multiple points of view, "Just Like a Tree" begins with the perspective of one of the party's youngest participants before moving on to other narrative angles. Each section is devoted to various family and community members. Men, women, and children, old and young, black and white come together to focus on place, community, and change. Gaines's choice of using ten narrators instead of one anticipates his technique in *A Gathering of Old Men*, and once again illustrates his mastery of language and tone. His careful arrangement of point of view creates not only verisimilitude but also a significant subtext.

The story takes place during a heavy rainstorm, and Chukkie's narrative focuses attention on the natural forces that make getting to Aunt Fe's cabin so difficult. Aside from the rain and consequent mud, there is the lazy mule, Mr. Bascom. This animal, a remnant of the past, refuses to carry his load and makes more work for Big Red and Chukkie's father, Emile. Later we will discover that Mr. Bascom holds a special place in the life of Emile's mother, Aunt Lou, reason enough for her to try to protect him from punishment. Emile, however, believes that all forces are against him, including his own mother. Though he shows respect for the past, he eyes a new tractor with longing, suggesting a certain eagerness to abandon some practices. When Gaines counterpoises the mule with the tractor, he suggests that change has already arrived at this plantation, threatening the tightly knit community where kinship isn't simply a matter of blood.

Aunt Fe is the spiritual center of the community. As its oldest surviving member, her name is as familiar to everyone as if she were family. In fact, Leola says that Aunt Fe's name is "like the name of God" (227) and compares her to a tree that has been in the front yard all of one's life. Moving Aunt Fe will not simply place her in a new location. It will remove the community's binding force, its link to the past which is the gateway to the future. Later, Aunt Clo will expand the tree metaphor, pointing out that removing a tree leaves not one hole but two, one in the ground and another in the sky, playing on the bridge that trees form between the elements and Aunt Fe's link to the past and future. Old trees, she knows, do not successfully transplant, especially a human one like Aunt Fe. Taking her north will only damage her. However, Leola also knows that the taproot of an old tree never leaves. Something of Aunt Fe will remain. We see Aunt Fe's continuing influence on other characters who claim her, including Anne-Marie Duvall, the plantation owner, and Adrieu, who calls Aunt Fe her "nan nan" (229). Aunt Fe's role as a mother to the community underscores her nurturing role, part of which involves relating the stories of her people's struggle. Late in "Just Like a Tree," we will also learn that the civil rights activist Emmanuel, whose presence has sparked the bombing, has likewise been touched by Aunt Fe. She has told him his family history, including the fact that his grandfather was lynched. Instead of retribution, Aunt Fe has always counseled peace. Everyone there recognizes her as a wholly positive force, everyone but James, that is.

As the only outsider at this gathering, James has no emotional connection to others. To him, Aunt Fe is simply an "old chick" (230). James's narrative reveals that he feels as if he has been dropped into an alien place. He understands neither its language nor its customs, and characterizes its practices and people as "primitive" (230). Young, northern, urban, and hip, James's language and habits suggest a person who has done his best to ignore the past and its meaning. He fails to appreciate the dynamic of this gathering, its spirit of communal loss and its celebration of a person who has created community. Instead, James depends on bourbon to blunt his feeling. That he calls a product by name (Mr. Harper) and fails to call anyone else—including his own wife—by name suggests an inability to see beyond surface similarities as well as a lack of respect. In fact, James's attitude reflects a reversal of the values enacted by community members, who prize human connection above material goods. Finally, this attitude underscores James's isolation. His presence reminds readers that a quite different world exists outside this plantation community, one in which ideas of mutual support and individual recognition no longer exist.

James's character is counterbalanced by that of Anne-Marie Duvall. If he feels neither affection nor connection with the people honoring Aunt Fe, she believes herself bound to this same group by tradition and duty. She, too, is an outsider, though she never quite sees herself as such because she feels bound by place and history to enact a public display of respect and repayment. Anne-Marie's narrative suggests a woman emotionally tied to Aunt Fe, who has worked for the Duvall family as both cook and nurse. Clearly, she has a strong sense of *noblesse oblige*, arguing with her husband over driving a difficult road in a driving rainstorm. Saying that her father would have gone, Anne-Marie indicates her sense of obligation in a number of ways. She must present in person a token of her esteem, in this case a seventy-nine-cent scarf. This image merits scrutiny because it brings to mind the kerchief ordered worn by all women of color by the Spanish government in 1768 to differentiate black women from white (Dominguez, 25). More than simply a fashion accessory, the kerchief signifies social status, and Anne-Marie's parting gift underscores the master-servant relationship she has with Aunt Fe. Moreover, its cheapness suggests her continuing devaluation of its recipient, though Anne-Marie seems oblivious to this.

Her shallow feelings emerge more fully as she drives toward Aunt Fe's remote house. Wondering about why Aunt Fe's house is so inconveniently distant from her own, she concludes that it was "ordained" (239) rather than owning up to the fact that the Duvall family placed those cabins at a distance from the big house. In using both the passive voice and the word "ordained," Anne-Marie absolves herself of any personal responsibility. Indeed, her free association of events suggests a woman unable to reflect upon anything deeply. She pretends to envy the apparent freedom of a "little nigger girl" picking pecans (241), but fails to recognize civil rights activism as a much more effective means to freedom. Her apparently naive question when she reflects on the three deaths caused by the bombing is, "What do they want?" (241). She might be taking Aunt Fe a gift because her father would have, but Anne-Marie seems incapable of reflecting on why she might need to show gratitude. Throughout her narrative, Anne-Marie depends upon racial stereotypes, making her quite conscious of her conspicuous participation as the "white lady" at Aunt Fe's party. This sense of self-importance drives her forward to a display of grief, but whatever sincerity she expresses in her tears is quickly undercut by her fast departure from the house.

The story's remaining two narratives suggest both understanding and acceptance of change. As Etienne reflects on Emmanuel's civil rights activism, he notes the young man's nonviolence and credits Aunt Fe's influence on him. Etienne recognizes—as many do not—that Emmanuel's work will continue even without his presence. Etienne's ruminations on events mark a shifting in the lives of plantation residents, or rather a cycle of change. Aunt Lou's concluding narrative continues this image as she relates Aunt Fe's final hours. Aunt Fe is unequivocal in her refusal to leave the place where she has given her life. Thus, she sings her "termination" song, and dies quite peacefully in her own bed, having made peace with her God. Gaines's construction of these narrative perspectives recognizes and pays homage to the old ways. Aunt Fe, having carried the memories and history of her community, has helped to inspire the change that inevitably comes.

Bibliography

WORKS BY ERNEST GAINES

The Autobiography of Miss Jane Pittman. New York: The Dial Press, 1971; Bantam Books, 1972.

Bloodline. New York: The Dial Press, 1968; Bantam Books, 1970; Norton, 1976.

"Bloodline in Ink." *CEA Critic* 51.2 (1989): 2–12.

Catherine Carmier. New York: Atheneum, 1964; Random House, 1993.

A Gathering of Old Men. New York: Knopf, 1983; Thorndike, 1984; Vintage, 1984.

"Home: A Photo-Essay." *Callaloo* 1.3 (May 1978): 52–67.

In My Father's House. New York: Knopf, 1978; Norton, 1983; Vintage, 1992.

A Lesson Before Dying. New York: Knopf, 1993; Vintage, 1994.

"Miss Jane and I." *Callaloo* 1.3 (1978): 23–38.

"Miss Pittman's Background." *New York Times Book Review*, 10 August 1975: 23.

Of Love and Dust. New York: The Dial Press, 1967; Bantam Books, 1969; Norton, 1979; Vintage, 1994.

"A Very Big Order: Reconstructing Identity." *Southern Review* 26.2 (1990): 245–53.

WORKS ABOUT ERNEST GAINES

General

Babb, Valerie Melissa. *Ernest Gaines*. Boston: Twain, 1991.

Bevers, Herman. *Wrestling Angels into Song: The Fictions of Ernest J. Gaines and James Alan McPherson*. Philadelphia: University of Pennsylvania Press, 1995.

Bryant, Jerry H. "Ernest J. Gaines: Change, Growth, and History." *Southern Review* 10 (1984): 851–64.

———. "From Death to Life: The Fiction of Ernest J. Gaines." *Iowa Review* 3:1 (1972): 106–20.

Byerman, Keith E. *Fingering the Jagged Edge: Tradition and Form in Recent Black Fiction*. Athens: University of Georgia Press, 1985.

Estes, David C., ed. *Critical Reflections on the Fiction of Ernest J. Gaines*. Athens: University of Georgia Press, 1994.

Folks, Jeffrey J. "Ernest Gaines and the New South." *Southern Literary Journal* 24.1 (1991): 32–46.

Greene, J. Lee. "The Pain and the Beauty: The South, the Black Writer and Conventions of the Picaresque." *The American South: Portrait of a Culture*. Edited by Louis D. Rubin, Jr. Baton Rouge: Louisiana State University Press, 1980.

Hicks, Jack. "To Make These Bones Live: History and Community in Ernest Gaines's Fiction." *Black American Literature Forum* 11 (1977): 9–19.

Lowe, John, ed. *Conversations with Ernest Gaines*. Jackson: University Press of Mississippi, 1995.

Rowell, Charles H. "Ernest J. Gaines: A Checklist, 1964–1978." *Callaloo* 1.3 (1978): 125–31.

———. "The Quarters: Ernest Gaines and the Sense of Place." *Southern Review* 21 (1985): 733–50.

Shelton, Frank W. "A Gaines Gold Rush: A Review Essay." *The Southern Quarterly* 34.3 (1996): 149–51.

Biographical

Byerman, Keith E. "Ernest Gaines." *Dictionary of Literary Biography*, vol. 33, *Afro-American Writers: 1955–Present*. Edited by Thadious M. Davis and Trudier Harris. Detroit: Gale Research, 1984.

Davis, Thadious M. "Ernest J. Gaines." *African American Writers*. Edited by Valerie Smith. New York: Scribners, 1991.

Doyle, Mary Ellen. "Ernest Gaines' Materials: Place, People, Author." *MELUS* 15:3 (1988): 75–93.

Grant, William E. "Ernest Gaines." *Dictionary of Literary Biography*, vol. 2, *American Novelists Since World War II*. Edited by Joel Myerson. Detroit: Gale Research, 1978: 170–75.

Simpson, Anne K. "The Early Life of Ernest Gaines," *Louisiana Literature* 7 (1990): 71–87.

———. *A Gathering of Gaines: The Man and the Writer*. Lafayette: Center for Louisiana Studies, 1991.

Reviews and Criticism

Catherine Carmier

Davis, Thadious M. "Headlands and Quarters. Louisiana in *Catherine Carmier*." *Callaloo* 7.2 (1984): 1–13.

Griffin, Joseph. "Creole and Singaleese: Disruptive Caste in *Catherine Carmier* and *A Gathering of Old Men*." *Critical Reflections on the Fiction of Ernest J. Gaines*. Athens: The University of Georgia Press, 1994.

Review of *Catherine Carmier*. *New York Times Book Review*, 14 June 1981: 86.

Review of *Catherine Carmier*. *New York Times Literary Supplement*, 10 February 1966: 97.

Stoelting, Winifred L. "Human Dignity and Pride in the Novels of Ernest Gaines." *College Language Association Journal* 14 (1971): 340–58.

Of Love and Dust

Blackburn, Sara. Review of *Of Love and Dust*. *Nation*, 5 February 1968: 185.

Granat, Robert. "Loner on Olympus." *New York Times*, 19 November 1967: 83.

Review of *Of Love and Dust*. *New York Times Literary Supplement*, 1 August 1967: D17.

Smith, David Lionel. "Bloodlines and Patriarchs: *Of Love and Dust* and Its Revisions of Faulkner." In *Critical Reflections on the Fiction of Ernest J. Gaines*. Athens: The University of Georgia Press, 1994.

Wideman, John Edgar. "Of Love and Dust: A Reconsideration." *Callaloo* 1.3 (1978): 78.

Bloodline

Burke, William. "*Bloodline*: A Black Man's South." *College Language Association Journal* 19 (1976): 545–58.

Callahan, John F. "Hearing Is Believing: The Landscape of Voice in Ernest Gaines's *Bloodline*." *Callaloo* 7.1 (1984): 86–112.

Duncan, Todd. "Scene and Life Cycle in Ernest Gaines' *Bloodline*." *Callaloo* 1.3 (1978): 85–101.

Gaudet, Marcia. "The Failure of Traditional Religion in Ernest Gaines' Short Stories." *Journal of the Short Story in English* 18 (1992): 81–89.

Griffin, L. W. Review of *Bloodline*. *Library Journal*, 93 July 1968: 2689–90.

Hicks, Granville. "Sound of Soul." *Saturday Review*, 17 August 1968: 19–20.

La Fore, Lawrence. "Various Vehicles." *New York Times Book Review*, 29 September 1968.

Luscher, Robert M. "The Pulse of *Bloodline*." In *Critical Reflections on the Fiction of Ernest J. Gaines*. Athens: The University of Georgia Press, 1994.

McDonald, Walter R. " 'You Not a Bum, You a Man': Ernest J. Gaines's *Bloodline*." *Negro American Literature Forum* 9 (1975): 47–49.

Pecile, Jordon. "On Ernest J. Gaines and 'The Sky Is Gray.' " *The American Short Story*, vol. 2. Edited by Calvin Skaggs. New York: Dell, 1980: 452–58.

Roberts, John W. "The Individual and Community in Two Short Stories by Ernest J. Gaines." *Black American Literature Forum* 18 (1984): 110–13.

Shelton, Frank. "Ambiguous Manhood in Ernest J. Gaines's *Bloodline*." *College Language Association Journal* 19 (1975): 200–209.

The Autobiography of Miss Jane Pittman

Andrews, William L. " 'We Ain't Going Back There': The Idea of Progress in *The Autobiography of Miss Jane Pittman*." *Black American Literary Forum* 11 (1977): 146–49.

Beckman, Barry. "Jane Pittman and Oral Tradition." *Callaloo* 1.3 (1978): 102–9.

Byerman, Keith E. "A 'Slow to Anger People': *The Autobiography of Miss Jane Pittman* as Historical Fiction." In *Critical Reflections on the Fiction of Ernest J. Gaines*. Athens: The University of Georgia Press, 1994.

Callahan, John E. "Image-Making: Tradition and the Two Versions of *The Autobiography of Miss Jane Pittman*." *Chicago Review* 29.2 (1977): 45–62.

Doyle, Mary Ellen. "*The Autobiography of Miss Jane Pittman* as a Fictional Edited Autobiography." In *Critical Reflections on the Fiction of Ernest J. Gaines*. Athens: The University of Georgia Press, 1994.

Fuller, Hoyt W. Review of *The Autobiography of Miss Jane Pittman*, by Ernest J. Gaines. *Black World*, October 1971: 87–89.

Gaudet, Marcia. "Black Women: Race, Gender, and Culture in Gaines' Fiction." In *Critical Reflections on the Fiction of Ernest J. Gaines*. Athens: The University of Georgia Press, 1994.

———. "Miss Jane and Personal Experience Narrative: Ernest Gaines's *The Autobiography of Miss Jane Pittman*." *Western Folklore* 51 (1992): 23–32.

Giles, James P. "Revolution and Myth: William Melvin Kelly's *A Different Drummer* and Ernest Gaines' *The Autobiography of Miss Jane Pittman*." *Minority Voices* 1.2 (1971): 39–48.

Maddocks, Melvin. Review of *The Autobiography of Miss Jane Pittman*. *Time*, 10 May 1971.

Pettis, Joyce. "The Black Historical Novel as Best Seller." *Kentucky Folklore Record* 25 (1979): 51–59.

Walker, Alice. "*The Autobiography of Miss Jane Pittman*." *New York Times Book Review*, 23 May 1971: 6.

Wolff, Geoffrey. Review of *The Autobiography of Miss Jane Pittman*. *Newsweek*, 3 May 1971.

In My Father's House

Aubert, Alvin. "Self-Reintegration Through Self-Confrontation." *Callaloo* 1.3 (1978): 132–35.

Burke, V. M. Review of *In My Father's House*. *Library Journal*, 1 June 1975.

Holloway, Karla F. C. "Image Act, and Identity in *In My Father's House*." In *Critical Reflections on the Fiction of Ernest J. Gaines*. Athens: The University of Georgia Press, 1994.

McMurtrey, Larry. Review of *In My Father's House*. *New York Times Book Review*, 11 June 1978: 13.

Review of *In My Father's House*. *Newsweek*, 29 May 1978.

Shelton, Frank. "*In My Father's House*: Ernest Gaines After Jane Pittman." *The Southern Review* 17:2 (1981): 340–45.

Watkins, Mel. "Books of the Times." *New York Times*, 20 July 1978: 13.

White, Daniel. " 'Haunted by the Idea': Fathers and Sons in *In My Father's House* and *A Gathering of Old Men*." In *Critical Reflections on the Fiction of Ernest J. Gaines*. Athens: The University of Georgia Press, 1994.

A Gathering of Old Men

Callahan, John F. "One Day in Louisiana." Review of *A Gathering of Old Men*, by Ernest J. Gaines. *New Republic*, 26 December 1983: 38–39.

Forkner, Ben. Review of *A Gathering of Old Men*. *America*, 2 June 1984: 425.

Harper, Mary T. "From Sons to Fathers: Ernest Gaines' *A Gathering of Old Men*." *College Language Association Journal* 31:3 (1988): 299–308.

Luneau, Teresa. Review of *A Gathering of Old Men*. *Saturday Review* 9:61 (December 1983).

Price, Reynolds. "A Louisiana Pageant of Calamity." *New York Times Book Review*, 30 October 1983: 15.

Rickels, Milton R. and Patricia Rickels. " 'The Sound of My People Talking': Folk Humor in *A Gathering of Old Men*." In *Critical Reflections on the Fiction of Ernest J. Gaines*. Athens: The University of Georgia Press, 1994.

Shannon, Sandra G. "Strong Men Getting Stronger: Gaines's Defense of the Elderly Black Male in *A Gathering of Old Men*." In *Critical Reflections on the Fiction of Ernest J. Gaines*. Athens: The University of Georgia Press, 1994.

Washington, Mary Helen. Review of *A Gathering of Old Men*. *Nation*, 14 June 1984.

A Lesson Before Dying

Babb, Valerie. "Old-Fashioned Modernism: 'The Changing Same' in *A Lesson Before Dying*." In *Critical Reflections on the Fiction of Ernest J. Gaines*. Athens: The University of Georgia Press, 1994.

Ruben, Merle. Review of *A Lesson Before Dying*. *Christian Science Monitor*, 13 April 1993.

Senna, Carl. Review of *A Lesson Before Dying*. *New York Times Book Review*, 8 August 1993.

Sheppard, R. Z. Review of *A Lesson Before Dying*. *Time*, 29 March 1993.

Other Secondary Sources

Baker, Houston A., Jr. *Black Literature in America*. New York: McGraw Hill, 1971.

Bressler, Charles E. *Literary Criticism: An Introduction to Theory and Practice*. Englewood Cliffs: Prentice Hall, 1994.

Cirlot, J. E. *A Dictionary of Symbols*. New York: Philosophical Library, 1971.

Dominguez, Virginia R. *White By Definition: Social Classification in Creole Louisiana*. New Brunswick: Rutgers University Press, 1986.

Forster, E. M. "The Plot." In *Approaches to the Novel*. San Francisco: Chandler Publishing Co., 1961.

Murfin, Ross C. "What Is Feminist Criticism?" In *The Scarlet Letter*, 275–84.

———. "What Is the New Historicism?" In *The Scarlet Letter*, 330–41.

———. "What Is Psychological Criticism?" in *The Scarlet Letter*. Edited by Ross C. Murfin. Boston and New York: Bedford Books of St. Martin's Press, 1991: 223–33.

Shor, Ira. "Notes on Marxism and Method." *College English* 34:2 (November 1972).

Wasson, Richard. "New Marxist Criticism: Introduction." *College English* 34:2 (November 1972).

Index